DON'T STOP ME NOW

Vassos Alexander

BLOOMSBURY

LONDON · OXFORD · NEW YORK · NEW DELHI · SYDNEY

This is for Caroline, Emily, Matthew and Mary. Who are everything.

Bloomsbury Sport
An imprint of Bloomsbury Publishing Plc

50 Bedford Square
London
WC1B 3DP
UK

1385 Broadway
New York
NY 10018
USA

www.bloomsbury.com

BLOOMSBURY and the Diana logo are trademarks of Bloomsbury Publishing Plc

First published in 2016
This B-format edition published in 2017

British Library Cataloguing-in-Publication Data
A catalogue record for this book is available from the British Library.

ISBN: Print: 978-1-4729-2154-3
ePDF: 978-1-4729-2152-9
ePub: 978-1-4729-2155-0

2 4 6 8 10 9 7 5 3

Typeset in Chaparral Pro by Deanta Global Publishing Services, Chennai, India
Printed and bound in Great Britain by CPI Group (UK) Ltd. Croydon, CR0 4YY

MIX
Paper from
responsible sources
FSC® C020471

To find out more about our authors and books visit www.bloomsbury.com.
Here you will find extracts, author interviews, details of forthcoming
events and the option to sign up for our newsletters.

Foreword

CHRIS EVANS

Vassos Alexander is an extraordinary human being. His Dad also has the finest, firmest, happiest and most committed handshake I have ever had the pleasure of being on the other end of. Energy and what to do with it are obviously deeply rooted in the Alexander gene pool. As a result of which Vassos simply has to exercise for a huge amount of his waking hours otherwise he might explode all over his beautiful wife Caroline and gorgeous and exemplarily well-behaved offspring Matthew, Emily and little Mary (who by the way could all run before they could walk and are already smashing their own PBs at weekly parkruns).

The result of this is our man Vass often turning up to work with a sweaty top lip at Radio 2 where he presents the sport on my Breakfast Show. The few droplets of glistening perspiration however, are the only real evidence of any extreme physical exertion. Bear in mind his commute often involves needlessly extended runs and cycles in various attempts to break his own personal bests between Barnes and New Broadcasting House.

But of course this is not Vassos actually exercising. That comes later in the day, via a 10-, 20- or 30-mile run depending on how he's feeling, how much time he has spare or what he might be training for at the time. The man is a phenomenon of calorie burning. Recently, during a 'thank you to my amazing team for putting up with me' trip to France, he'd run 50k before I'd even arrived from the airport, which he then followed with a one-mile pre-lunch swim and a display of truly fearless diving off the 10-metre-high sky deck of Eddie Jordan's old motor yacht *The Snapper*.

And so here he is now encroaching on my territory, having written a book about putting one foot in front of the other at various speeds and seeing where that can get a person and how it can make us feel. Encroachment eventually turned out to be mutual, as half way through his endeavour to get his running thoughts, experiences and encounters down on paper, I secretly took it upon myself to run the London Marathon.

I had become the first recorded human case of being infected by fitness from another person. Just being in the same studio for three hours a day, five days a week, forty weeks a year had been enough for him to infect me with energy, purpose and a goal that would change my life more profoundly and positively than anything I have ever done before.

He knows his stuff when it comes to running. His is the most authentic messenger of the art of running you could ever read. There are some amazing books, and I think I may now have read all of them, already written about what I do a bit and he does a lot. I am certain this tome is about to join the very best of them.

He's also a thoroughly good human being. But then I've never met a runner who isn't. It goes with the miles.

🌀 Bruce Springsteen, *Born to Run*

'OUTLAW' IRONMAN TRIATHLON, MILE 1

My body is at war with itself.

Every step is surprisingly excruciating. Of course having just swum 2½ miles and cycled 112, you wouldn't expect running to be easy. But I've trained hard for this. Almost every day for four months, I've forced myself to go for a run straight after a long bike ride – and nothing has prepared me for feeling as desperate as this.

My legs are like lead. It's not just a struggle to put one foot in front of the other; it genuinely takes every ounce of effort just to stay standing up. My right calf is screaming at me to stop. It began hurting early this morning, just after I started on the bike, and it's been getting steadily worse for five hours. I'm almost certainly doing myself some proper damage. Meanwhile my hip flexors have simply given up. They're not working at all, and seem to have downed tools and gone on strike in protest. I can't believe their timing; I've never needed them more. The only way to keep going without them is to twist left and right with every step – and that's starting to have a negative effect on my already-sore lower back. In fact, the hours in the saddle have seized up the muscles around my middle and forced me into a strange forwards-lean from the waist. I must look decrepit. I certainly feel it. My feet hurt, my neck and shoulders ache, my head is pounding, even my wrists are painful.

Yet all these issues pale into insignificance compared to whatever the hell is happening inside my gut. It's burning in there like I've swallowed a bottle of neat bleach. And the way it's throbbing must be how the Mexican boxer José Luis Castillo felt when Ricky Hatton knocked him out with that legendary body shot. It's also a constant, desperate struggle not to throw up. Every ten or fifteen seconds a tiny torpedo of bile shoots into my mouth, so every ten or fifteen seconds I somehow have to force it back down. But occasionally I fail, and some foul-smelling liquid dribbles down my chin and onto my running shirt.

I've run dozens of marathons before today, and never felt remotely as bad as I do now. Surely the only sensible thing to do is to stop running immediately, and find the nearest doctor.

And this is mile one. Compared to how I'll feel in an hour, this is a holiday.

You wouldn't describe me as an exceptional runner in any sense. I'm neither especially quick nor particularly graceful, although I suppose I can run a long way. And I try not to take myself too seriously when I run. So what follows is definitely not a celebration of my running ability – or inability – so much as a celebration of running itself. It's taken me on quite a journey, from my first pathetic efforts to make it to the end of my street to completing ultra-marathons and triathlons in the same weekend. And all I did was simply stick with it. Amazing really what a difference running, just plain old running, can make. Life-changing and life-affirming. A happy emoji.

I didn't start running because I gave up smoking, and I didn't stop smoking because I started running. The two just seemed to happen at about the same time, and each probably fuelled the other. That, and the fact I was starting to get a bit fat.

It began on my way to work after an early round of golf. I was looking forward to an afternoon reading the sports bulletins on Radio 5 live, happened to glance down and noticed what can only be described as a spare tyre, an alarming tube of fat about an inch wide, wrapped in a yellow golf shirt and flopping over my belt. I'd never considered myself to be anything other than slim before now, but suddenly realised I might need to re-evaluate. Because there it was, unmistakably. Fat.

I called my wife.

'Caroline, am I getting fat?' Caroline and I have been together since we were teenagers and she's usually really nice about this sort of thing. Wouldn't want to hurt my feelings. Wouldn't want to hurt anyone's feelings come to that. She's the sort of person who only sees the good stuff. So her answer came as something of a small electric shock.

'Well... (awkward pause)... I still think you're great... and it's completely normal to add a bit of ballast.'

It was true then. I was genuinely getting fat. It was bound to happen I guess. When you hit your mid-thirties, either you eat less, exercise more – or expand outwards.

Admittedly that last option was quite tempting. I remembered a conversation I had with the veteran sports journalist Steve Bunce during a late-night drive from Oxford to London. 'Let me tell you something Vass,' he intoned in his inimitable North London bark, 'I'm getting older, I'm getting wiser, I'm getting fatter... and I'm getting happier.' Well who doesn't want to 'get happier', even if it does mean buying some new, elasticated trousers? So yes, going the fat/happy route was kind of tempting. I could simply forget about that unseemly bit of flab hanging over my trousers, perhaps stop to buy a chocolate bar and a packet of crisps, and continue on my merry way to Television Centre safe in the knowledge I was merely relaxing into an older, wiser, happier middle age. And it would have involved a good deal less sweat than the route I chose.

I arrived at work on that inconspicuous Tuesday in October, and midway through an afternoon looking ahead to England's Euro 2008 qualifier against Estonia, snuck outside for a cigarette and a chat with my producer friend Jim. As always, I was armed with a frothy coffee and the obligatory packet of Frazzles.

Jim didn't actually smoke, and neither was he particularly overweight, but you could scarcely have described him as someone at the peak of physical fitness. Most weeks, after finishing our shift at half past six, he and I would head for a bit of a session in the on-site BBC bar. We could comfortably get through five pints and as many packets of crisps before calling it a night. Neither of us did any exercise (if you don't count golf – and frankly, with the best will in the world, you can't), we both ate badly, drank too much and we'd both left our twenties far behind us.

So on that autumn afternoon, during a break between bulletins, we decided something had to be done. We goaded each other, set our sights ridiculously, unrealistically high. One day, we vowed, we'd run a marathon. It seemed completely ludicrous – and it was exactly the sort of ambition I'd usually aspire to one day, and cheerfully forget about the next. But something about this stuck. I popped my head into the TV Centre gym on the way to the bar that night. The two were literally seconds away from each other – in fact you had to walk past the gym to get to the bar – and a good thing too, as I don't think I'd have bothered if it weren't so convenient. But I did go in, albeit a little apprehensively, and found myself booking an appointment for the following morning with an amiable physical trainer called Andrew. He's almost as wide as he is tall, Andrew, but it's all muscle. I awoke the next day to a slight hangover, and was tempted to call and cancel. But that would have meant sneaking past the gym like a naughty schoolboy every time I wanted a pint. Plus, Andrew's arms were wider than my legs.

On my way to that first session, I drank a can of Red Bull believing the various stimulants might help ease the pain. Andrew took my pulse and almost called a halt there and then; my heart rate was through the roof. But I persuaded him it must be the caffeine, and the torture began. First up, 20 minutes on the treadmill.

Paula Radcliffe MBE

Marathon World Champion and women's world record holder. Her time of 2 hours 15 minutes and 25 seconds is widely considered to be the greatest distance run by anyone, ever.

I don't really remember a time when I wasn't running, so I don't really remember my first actual run. But I was always joining in. My dad was running marathons for fun. I guess he ran at school, gave up, smoked at university, gave up smoking, put on a lot of weight, and took up running again to lose the weight around the time I was born. So I remember him always getting ready for London marathons, Mersey marathons and other races.

And when he was training we used to go to the forest. We lived near Delamere Forest in Cheshire and we used to go along, basically to give him a drink on his long runs. I also used to join in with him for small sections of his runs. They always seemed like a long way at the time, though it was probably only about half a mile.

Then I had a friend at school who was in the local athletics club and I knew you had to be nine to join that. So as soon as I was nine, I remember my dad took me down there and I joined Frodsham Harriers. I instantly knew I loved it, I instantly knew this was something I enjoyed, but I wasn't instantly much good! I wasn't bad, but I guess when I started I was just average.

In fact, in the early stages I tried everything: high jump, long jump, sprinting... But I knew that the longer stuff – the 800m and cross country – was what I enjoyed the most.

When I was 11 we moved to Bedford, and my dad did some research into the local clubs. He decided Bedford and County was the best option so he took me down there, and that's when I met Alex and Rosemary Stanton who became my coaches.

I used to do judo as well as athletics before we moved. But in Bedford I decided I much preferred the running, so I asked my mum if I could drop the once-a-week judo sessions and go twice a week to the track. She agreed, and it all built up from there. I was very fortunate that it was a good group and they were great coaches – under Alex and Rosemary I really started to just move through.

But at that stage I think it was as much the social side of it as the running that kept me interested, kept me keen. That, and the fact that the team was doing so well at the time. The women's and girls' sections of Bedford and County became amongst the strongest in the country, in spite of the club's relatively small size.

Initially though, our success was nothing to do with me. When I first started, I went to the national cross country and I came 299th. That was in the under-13 girls, and I was admittedly one year younger so I would have been 11 or just turned 12. After that Alex decided he was going to try to get the team to win the nationals the following year, so he went to talk to my mum. He said to her, 'I'm trying to get a group of six girls together to win the nationals next year, and Paula is one of them. Please can she come training an extra day a week, including one day at the weekend – so we can train to try to do this?'

And mum was great. She just said, 'Why are you asking me? It's Paula's decision; it's her you need to ask.'

And of course I did want to go more frequently, and in the same race the next year I was the second scorer in, and finished fourth. And we did win the team. After that we were always in the top three and I was always there or thereabouts. But in fact I didn't actually win the national cross country until I was 17.

These days I have moments when I simply love running, when I'm out on a run and realise there's nothing I'd rather be doing. But there are also days when simply getting one foot in front of the other is an issue. When you train hard there are always going to be tough times when you almost need to just switch off, or literally just focus on one foot in front of the other to keep going.

But then there are days when time passes really quickly, and it's my time to think and get my head in order. Sometimes when I run, that's when I think things through, and sort things out in my mind. But sometimes I'm running and thinking about nothing at all and I'm just in the moment, enjoying the experience.

Certainly after my foot injury, ahead of my farewell marathon in London in 2015, there have been lots of days when it's just one foot in front of the other just to make sure I'm running correctly. But then suddenly things will just click and it'll feel like it used to and I'll be running along simply enjoying the run.

I don't remember the first time I was ever on a run and suddenly thought, 'I'm really loving this' – but what I loved from the very beginning was that sensation of feeling alive and being in tune with everything.

And if I look at my kids now I can already see it in Raphael, who's five. Obviously he's not training or anything, but when he's running around, just the way he runs, I can see in his eyes that he's getting the same buzz from it. Isla is three years older, and by contrast she just runs because she's competitive, not because she loves the feeling.

Whether they want to follow in our footsteps or not (my husband Gary is a former Northern Ireland 1500m runner) I'll leave up to them. But I think being involved in sport is really important. From all the work I've done with kids and also from my own experience, you're more self-confident and you do better at school, you feel better about yourself, you're more in tune with yourself, you're generally a better person and a healthier person if you're involved in sport.

So will I encourage my kids to become involved in sport? Yes I will, but which one they choose is completely up to them. Because it has to be the one that lights up the passion inside them, and gives them the same enjoyment that running did for me.

And obviously, if they do choose running, I'll love it!

2

🎧 One Direction, *Ready to Run*

'OUTLAW' iRONMAN TRiATHLON, MiLE 2

I'm generally quite easy-going and not much fazes me. Sometimes I can even be a bit steely. I once flung myself behind a horse which was about to kick my elder daughter, took the full force in my shin – and pretended it was all a big, funny joke so that a four-year-old girl wouldn't develop a phobia of horses. Every morning I broadcast to 10 million people without missing a heartbeat. I've swum in the North Sea without a wetsuit in winter. Out of choice. I've been mugged at gunpoint in Johannesburg and was fine to continue broadcasting within minutes. But right now, on a sunny summer Sunday by a lake in Nottingham, surrounded by family, friends and well-wishers, I just want to curl up and cry.

This is mile 2. And I've just realised it's only going to get worse.

Every year a few hundred lunatics embark on a week-long race across the sand dunes of the Sahara desert. They carry all their own equipment, they tend to their own injuries (you should see the state of their feet), and in 50-degree heat they cover approximately the distance of a marathon every day for six consecutive days. Ask anybody who's run a marathon how their legs feel the following morning. It's nigh-on impossible to walk downstairs without wincing, most attempt to do it backwards. Now imagine how much worse your legs would feel after running 26 miles in the desert.

It's not just the heat that saps your energy: it's landing on loose sand, making you work hard for every single footstep. You'd wake up after that and have trouble simply standing up. So what would your legs be like if, somehow, you managed to persuade them to go through the same again, to run another 20-odd miles over the Sahara, 24 hours after doing it for the first time? Then imagine doing it for a third straight day, in the heat and the sand. And then on the fourth day casually double the distance, an ultra-marathon, still carrying all your own food and equipment. What state would your legs be in when you woke up on day five? And your legs aren't even your biggest problem. They're not even in the top two. More pressing is the state of your feet, bloody and swollen with nails missing and blisters on top of blisters. And most urgently of all, you somehow have to keep your mind positive enough to do it all over again after breakfast, to run another sapping, sandy marathon knowing you've got yet another in front of you tomorrow.

Meanwhile, every summer in the Lake District, a few dozen lunatics embark on a personal 24-hour crusade up and down 42 different mountains, or fells. Being in the extreme northwest of England, the weather is generally diabolical; freakishly strong winds carrying horizontal hailstones are not unusual. The runners do all their own navigation, frequently getting lost in thick clouds, which can appear from nowhere. They force their way up steep, seemingly impossible slopes totalling around 27,000 feet. They hurl themselves down dizzying descents in total darkness over loose stones, thick gorse and hidden boulders. Assuming they don't get lost and run further than necessary, which most do, it's about 72 miles of unrelenting slog. And if they finish one second over the 24-hour time limit – then quite simply, they've failed.

I'm guessing you may have heard of the Marathon des Sables in Morocco, but perhaps you're not aware of Cumbria's Bob Graham Round. Both events are currently very much on my 'to-do' list.

In fact I'd have run the Marathon des Sables last year if my wife hadn't forbidden it on the entirely reasonable grounds that she was seven months pregnant and could do without the added stress. And as for the Bob Graham, well I'm becoming increasingly obsessed with it since visiting Keswick, running in the fells, and meeting perhaps the greatest fell runner of them all, Joss Naylor. It's no exaggeration to call Joss a legend. And I don't use the term lightly.

He runs in the fells beyond the point of exhaustion, beyond the point of serious injury, beyond sleep deprivation, and he simply keeps going. Extremely fast. Here is a man who was told as a child that his bad back would forever prevent him doing sport of any kind. A man who aged 18 had an operation on his knee, which went so badly wrong that he was warned he'd never walk without a limp. A man who was excused military service because of his poor health. A man who was advised to stop working on his farm for fear of doing himself irreparable damage. But despite all that, or perhaps because of it, here is also a man who has done more to introduce the world to fell running than perhaps everybody else combined. A man who has won so many races, and broken so many records, that to list them all becomes boring. A man who's raised countless thousands of pounds for charity. Who once stopped whilst leading a race to go and help a lamb in trouble on a neighbouring peak. A man who once ran 20 miles over a mountain to get to the start of a major fell race, calmly and clinically won it, and then ran 20 miles back over the same mountain to be home in time to tend to his sheep.

And here is a man who celebrated his 60th birthday by leaving his house at 3am, running up and down 60 peaks, the equivalent of climbing Everest from sea level twice, and finishing 36 hours later in a faraway, lakeside car park – to the utter bewilderment of a group of tourists back from a Sunday afternoon hike. Iron Joss they call him. And they're not wrong.

And having met him, interviewed him, shared a pot of tea with him, I admit I'm a little star-struck. Not to mention obsessed with the challenge of completing a Bob Graham Round myself. Joss once managed 72 peaks in 24 hours, but the traditional 42 will do me. In fact it was Joss who inspired me to do my first off-road ultra-marathon, the

100km Race to the Stones, of which more later. And when I got to the start line and realised to my immense annoyance that I'd forgotten my running shoes (I mean what sort of total muppet *does that*?), I thought of Joss and carried on regardless.

But I'm getting ahead of myself.

Let's head back to my first, Bambi-like steps on a treadmill in Television Centre with Andrew, the personal trainer. When I set off, there were 20 minutes on the display, which I must have glanced at every five minutes or so to see how I was getting on. Except every time I looked up, only around thirty seconds had gone by. And according to the display, I was running quite slowly, yet it felt increasingly like I was sprinting. I complained loudly that there must be some mistake, was he sure the machine was working properly? Andrew simply stood by, patiently encouraging me in my makeshift sports kit to finish what felt like a 20-minute marathon.

The thing is, he kept telling me, once you've done 20 minutes or more of continuous cardiovascular exercise, your metabolism is fired up for the rest of the day so whatever you eat, you digest quicker and more efficiently. That's what he said, and as I've since learned, it's largely true. That's what he *said*. What I *heard* was, just keep running until this stupid timer reaches zero, and you can eat whatever you want with impunity for the rest of the week. Which is exactly what I did, via the half-hour of weights he made me do, and a quick shower. On my weary way downstairs for my shift that day, I gleefully visited the on-site sandwich shop for double portions of cheese ploughman's plus two packets of celebratory Frazzles. (Unfortunately I soon realised that if you're hoping to lose weight, it doesn't work quite like that.)

Fair to say I found my first proper exercise for over a decade quite a shock to the system. But somehow, I persuaded myself to return for more the following week. And the next week. And the one after that. And gradually, ever so slowly, week by week, month by month, I stopped viewing the treadmill (always the same one, the one in the corner, away from view) as the circle of hell that Dante had inexplicably forgotten to mention. I even began to wonder what it must be like to run outside.

Which is where I could be found quite soon afterwards, on my porch, trying to motivate myself to move.

The trouble is, running from home necessarily means running down my street, and potentially running in front of neighbours/friends/relatives/real people who actually know me. Which I found a little intimidating. So as I closed the front gate and turned towards the river, I set off at what can only be described as a flat-out sprint. If these people are going to see me run, I was thinking, then they're going to think I'm fast!

Of course a few dozen houses later, I was completely exhausted and found myself leaning against a friendly front wall to catch my breath. And that, sod's law being the sod that it is, was when the owner of that wall decided to leave her house along with a friend, both of whom I knew well. They did a collective double take as they saw me gasping for oxygen having clearly run no more than 200 yards.

Seriously quick thinking was required to spare me from weeks of ridicule. 'Just on my way home from a nice run,' I announced confidently. And in a classic case of protesting too much, added: 'I always finish my runs here, at the street lamp outside your house. Then I walk home as a warm-down.'

'Oh, we're all walking that way too,' came the unexpected answer. 'Let's all walk together.'

Nothing else I could do then, as we reached my front door, except confidently let myself back into the house. It was precisely four minutes since I'd proudly announced to wife and children that I was setting off on my inaugural outside run.

The ribbing I received was merciless, unremitting. And fully deserved.

And thus, with my three favourite people all enjoying themselves hugely at my expense, ended my first-ever proper run. It's a wonder I ever dared try again.

Joss Naylor MBE

'Iron Joss' is perhaps the greatest fell runner who ever lived. A sheep farmer from Wasdale Head, he's broken countless endurance records running in the Lake District but remains the most humble, unassuming and generous man you could ever hope to meet. He simply loves what he does (still does, even in his ninth decade) and where he lives.

When I first really got into running it was 1960, and it was the Mountain Trials at Wasdale Head. I was just having breakfast, and the proprietor there walked round to the counter where I was sat, and he said, 'Do you fancy running the Mountain Trial?'

I said, 'I don't know. I haven't got any running shoes. I haven't got any shorts. I've got nothing.' He said, 'You'll be all right.'

So I cut the legs out of my trousers and ran in my boots. I found it was the competition of running that I actually liked. I was going well, I was in the lead for about two-thirds of the way and then I got cramp. For about, I would say, an hour or so, I was struggling with cramp. I couldn't get rid of it. Just as we dropped towards Westmorland and one of the most beautiful views in the Lake District, there were two old ladies having a picnic. They had a little salt pot, so I said, 'Can I have some of your salt?' They said 'Yes, help yourself.' I turned half of it onto my hand and just ate it raw, and the cramp more or less went after that.

I finished the Mountain Trial, but I had very stiff legs the next day with having had the cramp. And that was my baptism to running. I always ran when I was at school and that sort of thing, but I never really thought about it till that day because there was no athletics in this area of any kind.

But then I really got into it. I've run the Mountain Trial, I think, over 50 times now. I still run it every year. You know, you get into something like that and, I don't say it exactly takes your life over, but it's something you look forward to each year because it's held at a different part of the Lake District. It's been a great way to discover the Lake District, a great baptism into this area – I've been into practically every inch of the Lake District with

Mountain Trials. And that's without doing the Wainwrights and things like that. [Joss once covered the famous Wainwright route – 391 miles, 214 tops and 121,000 feet of ascent – in 7 days, 1 hour and 25 minutes.]

And what I love about running I think is the tranquility. When you are running well and just floating along, it's one of those magical feelings. You can't really describe it. When you're running on a full stride and you're letting your feet drop, it's just something out of this world. It's one of those feelings that's pretty difficult to describe to people. A lot of people don't run right. If you're running at full stride and let your feet drop... your legs don't stiffen up the same. You get that sort of mythical sensation and you run and run and run, and just really enjoy it without taking a lot of energy out of yourself. You get to a certain stage of fitness and I just find myself thinking, well, how lucky I am to be here really. It's such a beautiful part of the world. We know the weather isn't always good in the Lake District, but even on a wet, bad day, those were the days I used to train because I couldn't get on to the other work, the sheep farming and that. If it was a bad day, I would always put plenty of thermal wear on the top – two good thermal tops and a light cap and it would be enough to keep your body heat without getting hypothermia or anything like that.

To anybody just starting out, I would say keep on the paths where you can't get lost. Learn to run on level places before you start climbing and just gradually work yourself into it. When you go out, gradually go a bit further – say every other week, add a mile to it. Concentrate on getting your climbing right. Just climb fast walking and then when you come to a bit of easy running, which is slightly uphill, just shorten your stride and try and run it. Try to keep a jog going until you do get to running on the hills, because it can be done so simply if you go about it in the right way.

And then improve slowly, run for longer. Because running for 24 hours in the fells, it's one of the great things. The night sessions, if you've got a good team with you, there's always a good craic and the time passes well.

It's magical because of the company you've got with you at night, and you rely on that company just to keep on track. It used to be a bit harder to see where you were headed, but nowadays there are some tremendous head torches. They run on a very small battery and the vision off them is magic. They weren't quite as good as that when I was doing the long runs on the fells. Now you see a lad coming at you at night, cycling, but when you first see the lights come you think it's a car. They light the whole road.

But I've seen some awful nights. When I did the 63 peaks [in 24 hours in 1975], it rained and stormed from start to finish, but apart from my face being a bit swollen with the rain and the wind, I took no harm at all. I just went home and Mary was milking the cows. And I said, 'I'll finish them off. You'll go and make the lads who've been out with me some breakfast.' Then I just worked all day.

◉ Kaiser Chiefs, *On the Run*

'OUTLAW' iRONMAN TRiATHLON, MiLE 3

We're running round the long, thin lake of the National Water Sports Centre at Holme Pierpoint near Nottingham. So far, I've managed to hobble up one of its 1½-mile sides, around the top, and now I'm heading back down the southern shore, back to where my wife and kids, if I can spot them among the crowds, will be waiting to cheer me on. It's mid-afternoon, and I reckon they'll have arrived up from London by now.

Over the past few weeks, Caroline has become increasingly anxious about today and has mounted a concentrated campaign to persuade me to pull out. For some reason, she's convinced herself that this Ironman could conceivably do me in. Perhaps it was the heart scare last year (which, having been sent for all the tests, rather shamefully turned out to be indigestion), or perhaps she's had a premonition. But the fact that this has turned into the UK's hottest day for years will have done little to calm her nerves. All around, there are some extremely fit, extremely well-prepared athletes collapsing with heat exhaustion and sunstroke.

Meanwhile, I've just spent two days in bed with a vomiting and diarrhoea bug, and didn't arrive in Nottingham until the early hours of this morning having helped to host the Radio 2 *Dine 'n' Disco* for Children in Need. Lovely day, mind you. A round of golf including a stunning exhibition of trick shots from world champion Paul Barrington. Another Paul, celebrity baker Hollywood, on hand to judge a Bake-Off. Not forgetting a boozy mid-afternoon Big Quiz, an amazing five-course dinner with a different Michelin-starred chef cooking each dish, and all topped off with a private concert from

Gary Barlow in the so-called Tipi of Love. Gary was just finishing his set when I forced myself into the car to start heading north. All great fun and for an excellent cause, but as a concerned Caroline pointed out on the phone – a fortnight of doing two jobs (a breakfast show as well as Wimbledon tennis commentary), followed by a bad attack of the runs, followed by a big charity bash, followed by hardly any sleep, represents less than ideal preparation for your first Ironman. Your first triathlon of any kind, come to that.

I'd also not had a chance to buy any proper kit, or even attach a water bottle to my bike. I was almost persuaded to turn back down the M1 except for one small thing. My sole accomplishment was having delivered my bicycle to the venue ready for the race, and the Outlaw's benevolent organisers, correctly suspecting my complete ineptitude and taking pity on me, promised to stick two water bottles onto my bike. Seemed rude not to race when they'd gone to the trouble. So I pressed on.

In fact, not that I know it as I trundle round the lake for the first time, my family were only a few hours behind me on the motorway. Caroline had the kids up at dawn, and they arrived hours ago.

They all witnessed me stagger off the bike and limp into the transition tent clutching my injured right calf. But as I head towards what (in several hours' time) will be the finishing line, I'm still labouring under the false impression that this is the first they'll see of me. There's calm water to my right, increasingly noisy grandstands to my left, and I'm determined to put on a show. Come on Vassos, grit your teeth and grin. As I reach the last of the grandstands, I attempt a burst of pace.

I promptly fall over.

Uh-oh. This is worse than I thought.

I've been running for about a decade and generally I absolutely love it. But to be honest, it does occasionally still take quite a lot of effort to force myself out of the house. Some runs feel tough, some feel like a chore, some seem unending, and some are slow and laboured. Some, but not most. Not even the large minority. And by contrast, I'll often find myself running somewhere stunning, the Lake District, say, or the South Downs, and my legs will feel epic, my lungs full, my core strong – and it seems like I can just go on forever. It's the best feeling in the world.

I've been trying to remember how long it took before I started to enjoy a run, any run, to any extent. Relishing the virtuous aftermath, that's the easy bit, it's instantaneous. As I never tire of telling anyone who'll listen – *you never regret a run*. But when do you start enjoying them?

I'm not sure you ever do have a bells and whistles 'Eureka' moment. I think what happens is you slowly start to embrace the fact that running has become part of your life. You appreciate that you're no longer out of breath after climbing the stairs instead of taking the lift. You welcome the slight burn in your legs which proves you ran hard yesterday. You relish having more energy in the morning, the fact that you need less sleep, that your libido seems higher. And mostly, *mostly*, you just love the fact that you can basically – not actually, mind you, but basically – eat whatever the hell you want.

For your first few runs, you do find yourself frequently glancing down at the watch wondering when you can reasonably start heading home. Then you begin to revel in the challenge of added distance and more time on your feet. But actually having fun? The first time I remember taking a moment to enjoy a run whilst in the thick of it was underneath the Malmo bridge just south of Copenhagen.

I'd been sent with a cameraman to interview the Sweden striker Henrik Larsson ahead of the Manchester United vs. Barcelona Champions League final (Larsson played for both clubs). At the time he was at Helsingborgs in his native country, a short drive from Copenhagen, where we landed late in the evening. After driving around aimlessly for a long while, we eventually found our hotel, which seemed to be located in the dead centre of nowhere. We switched off the engine and as the car lights went out, we found ourselves in total darkness. There was no other light, and no other car in the car park. There was also nobody at the reception desk and, as far as we could tell, no other guests. The entire hotel seemed completely deserted.

We double-checked, and yes, this did indeed seem to be the place the BBC had booked us into. Cameraman Andy mentioned that this was exactly the sort of set-up you'd find in a horror film, at which point we both privately became petrified.

Of course working for the BBC we were no strangers to spending the night in some ropey old places (some lovely ones too, I should add), but this hotel took the biscuit. It felt like we were extras in some Danish version of *The Shining*, and we half-expected Jack Nicholson to appear any moment wielding an axe. We seriously discussed heading back to Copenhagen and paying for an airport hotel out of our own money.

Ultimately, miserliness prevailed, and we managed to rouse someone on the phone who reluctantly came to check us in. He didn't look happy about the intrusion, and to be perfectly honest he didn't look entirely sane. Still, he thrust a pair of ancient-looking keys at us, waved us in what we assumed was the direction of our rooms and turned away.

But it turns out Andy is made of stern stuff, and wasn't going to be distracted from our overriding objective of the past few hours by the small matter of a psychopath receptionist in the Overlook Hotel's Danish sister. We were both starving, and he asked if there was any chance of some food. No chance at all, came back the brisk reply, along with a frankly murderous stare. You've got to hand it to Andy: if this was to be his last night on Earth, he was refusing to face it hungry. Anywhere round here we might find a shop then? No. A sandwich? No. Then could we possibly just get a slice of bread from the kitchen? No. No. And No. But eventually even Andy crumbled, and with stomachs rumbling and nerves still jangling, we retired to our spartan rooms. Sleep, when it came, didn't last long. The threadbare curtains weren't much good at their job so at 5am, as the sun rose over Scandinavia, my little room was flooded with bright light and I woke up. *At least I'm still alive*, was my initial conscious thought.

I got out of bed and shuffled to the window. What I saw through it moved me deeply. It turns out the hotel was situated in one of the most beautiful places I'd ever seen.

Impossible to believe that five hours previously I'd seriously feared for my safety! Here I was in a clean, cosy bedroom, looking out of the window at a blood-orange sun rising above an expanse of dazzling white sand and lush marshland. Beyond the mossy green acres was the icy blue Baltic Sea, and dominating the whole exuberant vista was the simply staggering Øresund Bridge (which at this point I'd never even heard of). Five miles long, double-tiered to take trains as well as cars between Sweden and Denmark, it's a vast, many-legged concrete arc standing proudly above the sea as it curves round to the right and out of sight over the horizon. In the centre, it's crowned by four colossal, triangular, cable-supporting towers. Magnificent.

Funny what some light does to alter the perspective. All of a sudden I was pleased the crummy curtains had got me out of bed a few hours earlier than planned. And I was doubly pleased to have thought to pack my running shoes. I left my room with a spring in my step, passed the same guy on reception who no longer looked menacing and even managed a sleepy half-wave as I skipped down the corridor.

Outside into the luminous morning, and away... At this stage of my running career, I'd rarely manage more than about 60 or 70 minutes before returning exhausted. But this morning I was delighted to have hours to play with if I wanted them. Which, I discovered, I did. I drank in the scenery, the solitude, the imposing man-made spectre above me. Enjoyed the fact that I had a job that allowed me, paid me, to come to beautiful places and run, before chatting to fascinating people. Enjoyed the fact that I felt strong and fit, that I wasn't in any hurry, and even – or perhaps especially – enjoyed the juxtaposition between the current feeling of near-euphoria and the ludicrous pantomime terror of the previous evening. I was probably out running for two hours, and it felt like a bit of a breakthrough.

Only a shame that the much-vaunted interview with Larsson was a little feeble in the end. A Swedish TV crew had also turned up to see him, but whilst I'd been out enjoying my morning exercise, they'd been busy artfully erecting a scaffolding backdrop with replicas of all his old club shirts draped from it (I mean, for heaven's sake!). They also brought along a leather trouser-wearing supermodel to conduct the interview. Henrik took one look at her, another at Andy and me, and decided to spend 56 minutes of his free hour with the Swedes.

We returned to Television Centre with a coupe of brief, lacklustre answers given as he walked back to his car. If only Henrik had known – we almost *died* to get that interview!

Steve Cram CBE

World 1500m Champion and Olympic Medallist. Once set three separate world records in 19 days. BBC Sports Personality of the Year, now a leading athletics commentator and presenter.

Right from the very beginning, what I loved about running was the idea that you do it on your own terms – you go as fast or as slow as you want to. That's one thing that really drew me to the sport. The other, obviously, was being quite good at it.

I'm pretty shallow, so anything I think I'm better at than other people, I instinctively like. I guess I'm also a bit selfish, and what hooked me early on was the contrast with the team sports we used to play. Unlike football and basketball, running isn't about the team. Running is all about me.

Growing up in Jarrow, we used to race round what we called The Block. It was a group of houses, probably about 400m all the way round. And one Sunday morning before lunch, when I was about nine or ten, we decided to change the rules a bit. Instead of racing round The Block once, we thought we would just run and keep going and going for as long as we could. See who dropped last. Well, the upshot is I won and won easily, and that's the first time I remember thinking, 'I'm a bit better at this than the other lads.'

So two years later when I went to senior school, and the first thing we did in games was cross country, I was actually looking forward to it. And I suddenly realised that running was something I loved. All the titles, all the medals, all the world records – they all started life on that Sunday morning in Jarrow.

I'm a recreational runner now. It's my relaxation as much as anything else, and when I'm running, I can just think. It's also the easiest way to keep fit. I travel a lot on the athletics commentary circuit, so I can simply pack my shoes and shorts and I'm away. And travelling widely as I do, running is a wonderful way of exploring new places, new cities, new routes. I don't listen to music as I go because when I run, I'm too busy taking in the environment.

Also, I never stress about my pace. But occasionally, if I'm somewhere like one of the big parks in London, people see me and think, 'Wow, it's Steve Cram – I'm going to overtake him.' So to be honest I prefer running where nobody knows who the hell I am.

And these days I often find myself out with fellow former international athletes who are as out of shape as I am – so I do wonder what people think when they see two or three of us out for a waddle. And in my case, it really has become a waddle.

We talk about the old days as we go. But the worst thing recently is Paula Radcliffe's decision to join the BBC commentary team. I've been out for two runs with her this year, and find myself just hanging on for dear life, saying nothing, hurting everywhere, letting her do all the talking.

⊕ Spencer Davis Group, *Keep on Running*

'OUTLAW' iRONMAN TRiATHLON, MiLE 4

Have I mentioned that it's hot? And I don't mean hot as in warm, pleasant, sunny, balmy, temperate, agreeable or lovely. Today is hot as in boiling, sweltering, blazing, burning, melting, scorching and stewing. Hot as in you'd think twice before ambling to the shops for an ice cream because you'd be too exhausted by the time you got there to enjoy your Cornetto. Hot as in you feel yourself burning in the shade despite the factor 50 you've just re-applied. Hot like the Sahara. Hot like a sauna... H O T!

So as I stagger into mile four, with almost 90% of this marathon still in front of me, I naturally start worrying about Andy Murray.

Because on this July afternoon whilst I'm trying to prove something to myself (not quite sure what exactly, but definitely something), Andy is 150 miles due south trying to win a tennis match. But not just any tennis match. He's on Centre Court at Wimbledon along with 15,000 fortunate fans and millions more watching on TV, playing and desperately trying to beat the Number One player in the world. He's also trying to win a cheque for £1.6m and overturn 77 years of British sporting history in the process. For the second time in 12 months, Murray stands one victory away from becoming a national hero, the first British man since the 1930s to win Wimbledon. And if it's this hot up here, I keep thinking, imagine how hot it is in London. And if I'm struggling with the heat and I'm Greek, how can Scottish Andy possibly be coping?

Silly, really, the lengths you go to take your mind off things. Another five miles, I decide arbitrarily, and I'll allow myself to find out the latest score from SW19.

Thirty seconds later I can't help myself.

'How's Andy Murray getting on?' I blurt to the nearest spectator.

'He's just broken the Djokovic serve in the first set!' comes back the cheerful reply.

Brilliant news, and just what I needed to hear. Right then, if Andy can do it – so can I. No more moaning about heat, injuries and stomach cramps. No more feeling sorry for myself. Onwards....

It's day one at my new school, and everyone is laughing at me. Even the Head. Especially the Head. In fact they went and found the Head with the express purpose of giving him a giggle at my expense.

I should explain.

I'd been to see a very clever sports doctor, Simon Kemp (who also looks after the England rugby team, and from whom more later), and he suggested I get my running gait analysed and improved to prevent further injuries. The place he suggested is called The Running School, located in an unassuming gym-like space underneath some railway arches in Chiswick, West London.

The Head in question is Mike Antoniades, and he might just be the world's leading expert on running technique. His interest in the subject was born when he had to retire from playing football because of a succession of knee problems. He simply couldn't understand why he'd recover from each injury, but still couldn't comfortably run. The specialists were equally baffled. All of this was long before the Internet, so Mike's only option was to start researching his problem in a library. He read every book he could get his hands on about the human nervous system, whilst simultaneously beginning to work with elite athletes.

'That's when I started noticing a link between running technique and what I now call *movement re-patterning*,' he tells me. 'So I began experimenting on myself, running 5k, 10k races, getting a lot of injuries in the process. Physiotherapists could treat the pain – but a huge part of rehab is returning to running correctly, so I started thinking about the cause rather than the symptom.'

It's now six years since my last visit as a pupil but I'm back at the Running School, chatting to Mike in a side room close to the treadmill where I'd once caused him so much mirth. I'm embarrassed, because he still remembers that original visit vividly. Apparently very few clients are as bad, as comically bad, as I was.

'You were interesting, to put it mildly. Totally, and I mean *totally*, uncoordinated limbs. These days I categorise runners – bad runners – into four groups. The Thumpers hit the ground really hard. The Shufflers barely lift their feet. The Slows could walk faster than they run – you often see them in the park at weekends. And you were an Octopus: arms and legs all over the place.'

What I went on to learn at his school is that running is almost as much about your arms as your legs. My trainer was a ludicrously fit man called Dan Baker (as opposed to Danny Baker, who I've also worked with and is much funnier, but who I'd hesitate to describe as ludicrously fit). Anyway, whilst giving me seemingly endless exercises to strengthen my core and improve my stability, Dan taught me to concentrate on my arms. As Mike puts it:

'Humans are cross lateral animals, so when we move the left leg, we also move the right arm. That's the way we were designed. If you haven't been taught that, and you don't have the background of skills, then you just run how you think is normal. And in some cases, and you were one of them, it's as if you've got four independent limbs going in four completely different directions.'

So how come some people seem to be able to run beautifully, gracefully, instinctively, whilst others, like me, need to go to school simply to avoid looking like an octopus? Mike has a theory on this too.

'A lot of people, and I suspect you were one of them [his suspicion is correct], didn't do much sport at school or at a young age. Everyone develops at different rates, and these kids lagged behind their peers in terms of certain gross motor skills*. And this kid, who is a slow developer, he can't catch or throw or kick as well as his mates, so he naturally shies away from sport – because he doesn't want to be embarrassed.

'Then suddenly the kid grows into his mid-thirties, and he starts getting fat. He decides to go for a run, and discovers he likes the way it makes him feel. And would you believe it? Our kid, now a man, finds out there's more inside him than he thought possible – a good pair of lungs, good mental strength – but what he doesn't have is any coordination between upper body and lower body. That's where we come in. And as you discovered, it takes about six weeks to change how the brain activates the muscles, through something I call a movement map. And hey presto, six weeks on, and you started running properly.'

To be honest, I'm still bristling from being described as an octopus. I once heard that the golfer Jim Furyk, genuinely good guy that he is, doesn't mind his swing being described, famously, as 'a man wrestling an octopus in a telephone box'. But I'm not as nice as Gentleman Jim, so I decide to retaliate – to test Mike's theories a little, see how he stands up to some Paxman-like questioning. Mike, answer me this. How come for every athlete who runs beautifully with a perfect gait, for every Mo Farah, there's a Priscah Jeptoo, who wins major marathons with knees collapsing inwards and ankles flailing outwards?

Mike enthuses: 'Actually, Mo is a good example. When his coach Alberto Salazar changed his arms, Mo was amazed at the difference it made to his speed. This is a world champion who at 28 years old moves his family to Portland where Salazar runs the Nike Oregon Project, and the first thing he does for six or eight weeks is work on his technique.'

---

* Gross motor skills are the abilities usually acquired during infancy and very early childhood as part of a child's physical development. These skills are improved and refined until adulthood. As the gross movements develop in a head-to-toe order, kids will typically learn head control, then trunk stability, and finally standing up, walking and running.

Mike is definitely right about that. Indeed, Mo admits that before he went to work with Salazar, his technique was questionable. And as a measure of how much he improved, consider the 2008 to 2012 Olympic cycle. On the final Saturday of the London Games, Farah won his second gold medal in the 5,000m. The stadium was so noisy that people in seats near the roof had to put their fingers in their ears. Except they weren't *in* their seats. They were standing up and cheering and yelling and beseeching Farah to dig deep and stay ahead of the two East Africans, Ethiopia's Dejen Gebremeskel and Kenya's Thomas Longosiwa, who looked like they were on the point of overtaking him throughout the agonising final lap. A final lap that took just 52 seconds by the way, and cemented Mo's place as an all-time great of British sport. Four years earlier in Beijing, he'd failed to even reach the final.

So what is so good about Mo's running gait? I mean, he looks like he's running on wheels and it's a thing of great beauty to behold, but there's also science behind the poetry. Experts have examined Farah from every angle, and having become a bit of a gait geek myself, I once compiled a list of what seemed to be the six key areas that make him so good. For what it's worth, and for the benefit of similarly obsessed runners, here's that list in full:

1. **No wasted energy**
The hips and shoulders stay level, while the legs move straight forward – making for a very efficient gait. Minimal energy is lost going sideways or up and down. There's also no sign of either knee collapsing inwards, even at the end of a race when fatigued.

2. **Hang time**
Nobody was ever injured in mid-air, so they say. And the 'stance' time, the amount of time the foot is in contact with the ground, is very short. Again, this minimises energy loss.

3. Mid-foot strike

When the foot does land, it does so with the ball rather than the heel. This reduces impact on the ground, essentially making for a run that's lighter on the feet.

4. Cadence

Not *how*, but *where* the foot lands: in this case just in front of the centre of gravity with the shin almost vertical – meaning minimal momentum is lost as the body travels over the foot to be ready to push off. This in turn allows for a high cadence, or leg turnover, increasing speed.

5. Arm swing

Yes we're back to the arms. They're unusually high, but bent at a perfect 90 degrees. This allows for excellent elbow drive.

6. And relax

Everything seems effortless: hands are open, shoulders loose and face muscles relaxed (compare and contrast to many athletes who clench their fists, hunch forwards and lock their jaws with the effort of it all). And as most sprinters will tell you, relaxed muscles go quicker than tense ones.

Having said all that, the greatest distance runner of all time, Haile Gebrselassie, had a kink in his technique, a crooked left elbow, which was a legacy of his childhood in Ethiopia where he used to run six miles to and from school every day carrying his textbooks under his arm. And back in Chiswick, Mike's avoided the question about Jeptoo. She's the Kenyan who came within five seconds of winning gold in the 2012 Olympic marathon. Eight months later she returned to the city and obliterated the rest of the field to win the London Marathon by over a minute.

Jeptoo is the first to admit that her style is idiosyncratic to say the least, even ungainly. However, she'll also point to her phenomenal success as a long distance runner and tell you that she gets away with it. So, Mike, perhaps you *can* run 'like an octopus' and win.

> Well it's actually quite simple. She's fast, but she could go a lot faster. And because of those knees buckling, sending her ankles flailing, she gets more than her fair share of injuries. So she runs a race, then she's out for ages, and that's basically down to her biomechanics. You would have thought someone would have told her, but I do a lot of work with elite coaches and their athletes, and it never ceases to amaze me how they don't look at what I call the bleeding obvious. So if one leg is moving this way, there has to be a counter movement because that is the way the human body works.

Jeptoo may disagree, but for me, Mike and his team were absolutely spot on. Not only have I rarely been injured since going to running school, but also, whenever I'm struggling on a long run and I can feel myself fading and my technique flagging, I simply remember to start pumping my arms, which seems to act as a trigger for everything to come together.

So as I bid farewell to Mike and leave the school for the final time, I can't resist a quick peek at the treadmill I was once taught on. There's another bloke on it now, clearly a new boy as his gait is all over the place. He's another octopus.

I stop for a moment and stare. I can't help a little smile. It does look funny; arms and legs swinging wildly in various directions. But give it a few weeks, and he'll be fine.

Donovan Bailey

Double Olympic champion, three times World Champion and 100m world record holder. For much of the nineties, he was the fastest man on the planet.

I never thought running was my thing. I was born in Jamaica, where track and field was certainly as big as football in the UK. I guess football's getting like that in Jamaica too now, but when I was young, it was like every single Jamaican child, at some point, is a runner. Or at some point is an athlete, because that's the easiest sport to do.

I grew up on a farm. There were only three things: it was school, church and sports. Those are the only things we did. I didn't grow up in an age of computers and all that stuff, so playing meant playing outside, and it was very important. Activities were very important. We ate well, but we were outside playing games. It might start out as early as when you first start to walk, just as little silly races, but then it grows from there.

We start school in Jamaica at three. When I was five I had my first sports day, and you kind of do a whole bunch of events. The ones I really enjoyed were the long jump, triple jump, and 100 and 200 metres. I probably discovered I had a special gift when I was about ten years old, again, at school sports day. I won a couple of ribbons, so I thought I was special anyway.

When I'm flying down the track, a lot of the time I don't think of anything. It's either absolutely nothing, or everything. I think that at speed, thinking is different. Sprinting is so very different to running. As a sprinter, when you're racing, there's not a whole lot to think about. You have to concentrate on your drive phase, when you explode out of the blocks, and then when you hit top speed, it's all about breathing. But essentially, you get up every day, and you do monotonous things to perfect every aspect of the sprint, to improve your drive, transition and speed, all for when you're actually on the track in a race. You're like an engineer constantly tinkering with a finely tuned sports car trying to coax more speed out of it.

I only understood that when I got to be professional. As a child, you're only really trying to run. Or actually, you're just trying to beat your opponents. But professionally, there are definitely phases in which you run. You have to understand gait. You have to understand your diaphragm. You have to understand breathing. You have to understand every single thing about your body. Living, breathing, and dedicating your focus and essentially your life, all of it to the sport. It can be difficult sometimes.

When I think back to the world records I've broken, those are probably the easiest races I ever ran. It's almost like your body's at one with the track, or with the environment around you. Maybe it's a zen state, or you're in the zone. Anytime I've ever gone and tried to run fast, it never happens. You have to understand, it really is the best feeling, when everything falls into place!

To me, looking back at the 1996 Olympic Games 100m final, breaking the world record and winning the gold medal, the way I would describe it... One, I thought I had a terrible start, which I did. But then, if I was to stand and look back at how I could see the crowd for instance, everyone just looked like an abstract painting. I came out of the blocks, and there was absolute silence – although, as we know, when you watch sport, the Olympic 100m final, the stadium is completely deafening, huge decibels of sound. But to me there was completely dead silence. And then when I crossed the finishing line, gold medal, world record, it's like the volume got turned up again.

Nowadays I stay in shape by playing a bit of basketball, a bit of golf, but last week I did a crazy thing. I decided to go for a 22-mile run, which as a sprinter, is just the worst thing in the history of the world. Yeah, it was good afterwards, but I am just not built for that. I'm completely built for speed. In fact I'm still hurting today. I'm hurting terribly today, so I definitely respect runners a lot more now.

⦿ Kanye West, *Runaway*

'OUTLAW' iRONMAN TRiATHLON, MiLE 5

It's sudden. Urgent. Desperate.

One second ago, literally one second in the past, everything was OK. By which I don't actually mean OK at all. I mean still agonising, exhausting, excruciating. But this is a new and utterly compelling problem that dwarfs all others: it's serious, distressing and needs sorting, like, *now*!

Oh, and I ought to say, I'm really sorry about what you're about to read. I apologise in advance. This is hardly the sort of thing you'd expect to find in a wholesome book about running. I mean for all I know, you could be about to eat your breakfast. I think breakfast is when you'd least like to read what's coming up, though lunch and dinner are a close second and third. So basically, I hope it's nowhere near any of your major mealtimes, and that you're generally OK with this sort of thing.

Because this is mile five, and as I say, it's sudden, urgent and desperate.

I need a poo.

This is not a gradual realisation, you understand. Or a mild pointer towards the closest convenience. This is the most abrupt, unforeseen and dramatic poo compulsion in human history. One moment I'm happily (well, not happily exactly, but you know what I mean) running along by the Trent, and the next – the Very. Next. Moment. – I'm horribly and acutely aware that I have *five seconds* to find somewhere to defecate, or else I'm going to soil myself.

Now of course I do know that marathon runners, especially (apparently) female ones, have long had to deal with similar problems. Indeed in one infamous case, live on television, hunched over on a kerb in central London.

But firstly, I've never previously needed so much as a wee during a marathon before. In fact during any run. And certainly never number twos. Also, and I'm clearly not speaking from experience here and research is a little tricky to come by, but from what I can gather, when the poo urge strikes mid-race, it tends to do so with a lot less drama and a little more forewarning.

So what to do in my current predicament? I now have four and a half seconds to find a makeshift toilet, which narrows my compass to around ten metres in every direction. Finding an actual public lavatory nearby, preferably a clean, unoccupied one, would be perfect. I look around me. Evidently not. Everything to my left is open parkland, where people are walking dogs, eating picnics, kicking footballs, generally enjoying a carefree Sunday afternoon. And there are kids about. I discount everywhere to my left immediately.

Three seconds remaining.

Immediately in front and behind me is the Trent towpath. Every few metres a would-be Ironman staggers onwards, either in the same direction as me, away from the National Watersports Centre, or back towards Holme Pierpoint (these runners are around ten miles closer to the finish than me, the lucky, speedy gits). Obviously, the actual towpath is a no-no as well.

Two seconds remaining.

Which leaves the area to my right, the few metres between the path and the river. The water isn't actually visible from where we're running, because there are thorn bushes growing luxuriously from the ground to about head height. They're thick, verdant, and extremely painful-looking. Doing a poo in there would be bottom suicide.

One second remaining.

I dive into the thorn bushes.

The skin on my legs and arms rips savagely as I try to get out of sight before tearing down my shorts and allowing the explosion to take effect. Even though I've had this problem for only a few short seconds, the relief is massive. Waves of sheer happiness wash over me as I deliver some unexpected compost to the thorn bush. If my feelings at the finish line are anything like as ecstatic as these, then the whole experience will perhaps have been worth it.

More skin ruptures as I exit the thorn bush sheepishly, but contentedly. Who cares about the cuts? I've dodged a bullet there. And as I continue on my way, I almost have a spring in my step.

By all rights, my brother-in-law should be more nervous than I am: he's with a load of strangers whilst I'm amongst friends. But the crucial difference is that he's been running for years and knows he's going to be OK today: he's seen it all before, done it all before – and then some. In fact he's done it all before – and then not just *some* but *same*, as in same again. Because David's already run a marathon, and this is just a half. Not even a proper half either, because the course is apparently too downhill to count as a bona fide half-marathon. So what I'm about to attempt, what I'm nervously contemplating, what kept me awake for much of last night is actually, officially, merely a 13.1-mile mass participation race. Or, if you prefer, the Great North Run. It's my first race of any description.

I'm especially nervous because for the year or so that I've been running, running is all I've talked about. At home, at parties, in the office, even on air, I've been evangelical about how brilliant running is, how I'm really enjoying getting out there, how I'm losing weight whilst gaining fitness and endurance. So people, understandably, have inferred that I'm quite good at it. I mean nobody goes on about something to this degree if they're not at least passably talented, right? And certainly my friends, colleagues and brother-in-law are all thinking that even if I'm not especially fast, then certainly I'm proficient enough to manage a measly half-marathon without too much trouble.

This is an erroneous impression I've done little (nothing at all) to correct. I rather like being thought of as a good runner. But I'm very much afraid that in the next few hours, I'm very publicly going to be unmasked.

Phil Williams, Radio 5 live presenter, Aston Villa fanatic, all round good guy, has organised the BBC team for the run. There are about a dozen of us in all, including Luke Harvey, jockey turned racing broadcaster, and George Riley, fellow 5 live sports presenter (at the time I worked on Breakfast, and George on Drive, so between us we had both ends of the day's sports news neatly wrapped up in three-minute bulletins). The entire station was out in force in Newcastle because the race coincided with one of the now defunct annual 5 live festivals, bizarrely called *Oktoberfests*, which were a fairly transparent attempt to boost listening figures in the North of England (Hull and Sheffield also got the *Oktoberfest* treatment). And somehow my brother-in-law, a headteacher on the south coast, has managed to infiltrate our running team.

Dave had dinner with us on the eve of the race. It was a very virtuous affair during which everybody ate a healthy, high-carb meal and nobody touched a drop of alcohol. Nobody, that is, except Luke, who cheerfully downed three or four lagers with his pre-race pasta and then proceeded to comfortably beat us all in the following morning's race. Dave meanwhile, who hadn't booked anywhere to stay for the night, managed to persuade me that my hotel room was big enough for both of us (which it wasn't).

Our race numbers were handed out, and I discovered I would be 909 to Phil's 693, the two medium wave frequencies of 5 live. And I also learnt that, apart from the look-at-me numbers, the organisers had laid on race chaperones for us both, experienced runners who would complete the route alongside us. Dave thought this was hilarious; it made me even more nervous.

I didn't sleep well that night, around 50% due to David's extraordinary snoring, and 50% down to nerves. I honestly had no idea whether I could get round 13.1 miles. I've just had a look at the list of runs I did to prepare for the race. I'm a little besotted with my running lists, so much so that I've made a note of every run I've ever done – and ahead of the Great North Run, it seems my longest training effort was an eight-miler the weekend before the race. I usually put a little comment by each run and that one, at 11am on a Saturday, was 'hard for the first hour then sort of OK. Very sore and swollen left knee after.' That pesky knee had been giving me grief on and off for months, and I genuinely had no idea whether it would survive the pounding it was about to take from Newcastle city centre all the way to the seaside at South Shields.

Over breakfast I'm quiet, unusually introverted. Then I'm shocked at how frequently I seem to need the toilet. Welcome to a race day! Next, another race ritual to experience for the first time – fumbling with safety pins. My inaugural attempts to attach a number to my running vest result in several painful holes in my thumb. I've never managed to get the hang of these. I've attempted the procedure many, many times since, and always seem to puncture myself in the process. Perhaps, when I finally persuade a race number onto a shirt without any form of self-inflicted injury, perhaps only then will I be able to say: I am a runner.

Not this morning though. This morning I'm just terrified.

Terrified of failing to finish, terrified of finishing in an embarrassingly slow time, terrified basically of being unmasked as a fraud.

There follows a lengthy walk to the start line during which I join in enthusiastically as everybody on the 5 live team tries to outdo each other with earnest tales of how little training they've done. I also tell anyone who'll listen how much my knee has been hurting. Blatant tactics: get the excuses in early. We reach the start, and I naively expend much of my seemingly limitless nervous energy running up and down the first few hundred yards of the course. Trouble is, because we're lucky enough to begin at the very front, the empty road stretches out invitingly ahead and almost begs to be run on. Tens of thousands of pounding feet are about to be released onto that tarmac, and this feels like making the first footprints on virgin snow. I just can't help myself.

My brother-in-law goes off to 'get his race head on' as I stop for a quick chat on air with Stephen Nolan. He's presenting the 5 live Weekend Breakfast programme from the start line. 'Why on earth would you want to put yourself through 13 miles of hurt?' he asks, entirely reasonably.

'For what I believe you Irish call the craic,' I lie smoothly, before adding – truthfully as it happens – that I'm also hoping to raise money for charity.

Despite the nerves, I have to admit that the atmosphere around the start line is intoxicating. Sure, people are edgy, jittery, jumpy. But they're also excited, happy, resolute and generous with genuine good wishes. It's a terrific place to be, overflowing with positive energy.

Minutes to go until the race is going to be officially started by Ant and Dec, and I meet Paul who's to be my chaperone. He's incredibly nice about being drawn to run with some bloke who broadcasts on a radio station he's never heard of, but having recently accompanied Nell McAndrew (beautiful, great company and a terrific runner with a marathon best of 2:54) round the Manchester 10k, I know he must secretly be a little disappointed.

Actually, speaking of a rough draw, and speaking of Ant and Dec, I was once with the pair of them at a charity golf day in Surrey. Eighteen teams of three players who'd each paid lots of money to play at a posh club with one of eighteen celebrities of wildly varying status – everyone from the nation's favourite TV presenting duo, to a Breakfast Show sports reporter who was there as a last-minute replacement. There would be a pre-round draw to match the 'celebrity' to the team. After 15 of the 18 names were picked out of a hat, the three that remained were Ant McPartlin, Declan Donnelly, and myself. Next to be drawn: *Vassos Alexander*. The unlucky team couldn't stop themselves letting out a loud, involuntary groan. However hard I subsequently tried to make it up to them for the five hours it took to complete the round, it was no use. No amount of indiscreet stories or tales of general sports reporting incompetence could make up for the fact that I was the unwanted 33% chance of not getting to spend the afternoon with either Ant or Dec. In golfing terms, they were two up with three to play, and lost.

But back to the Geordie duo at the start of the Great North Run, along with my chaperone Paul. He's chatty and charming as he asks what sort of time I'm hoping to achieve. Now at this point, surely, I should come clean about my running ability, or lack of it – but even here, on the start line of my first ever race, with no hiding place in front of me, just 13.1 unforgiving (though overall slightly downhill) miles,

I try it on. 'An hour and a half, or thereabouts.' This reply, optimistic in the extreme, is out of my lips before I can think straight, though I'm also eager to tell Paul about how injured I am in the knee department. I tell him that a lot.

The gun goes, fired by Ant or Dec or both, and we set off with a surge of adrenaline and excitement. Very soon, however, I am to learn another important race lesson (which again, I will blithely ignore in the future) – namely, that it's hard not to set off too quickly if you're fortunate enough to be invited to start at the front of the field. You spend the first few miles with all the genuinely fast runners surging past you, which makes you feel ridiculously slow. This in turn makes you speed up, and that's something you end up regretting when the going begins to get tough.

As it happens, the first few miles of the GNR are all pleasantly downhill – past the imposing St James' Park football stadium and out of the city across the iconic Tyne Bridge. The red arrows fly overhead, red white and blue smoke arching dramatically through the sky, and any pre-race anxiety over speed, injury and endurance simply evaporates like the coloured smoke overhead. Not even Paul's wise advice that we're running too quickly, that we're on for sub-80 minutes at this rate, can dampen my spirits. This is brilliant! This is easy!

Out of Newcastle now, and on towards Gateshead. The route is lined by thousands of loud, smiling, well-wishing supporters. There's a carnival atmosphere, families are out enjoying what must be quite a spectacle – a long, seemingly endless line of running, jogging, shuffling, determined humanity, much of it in fancy dress, all intent on the same distant finishing line. Kids hold out hands, hoping to be high-fived by the passing hordes. Generous locals have brought oranges, bananas or, best of all, Jelly Babies to give the runners a much-needed sugar boost. Everybody's smiling.

And in amongst all this positivity and joviality, that's when I start to labour. Paul is brilliant, keeping up an almost constant dialogue, first to keep me focused but very soon just to keep me moving forwards. I'm comprehensively struggling as the six-mile marker comes and goes, truly paying the price for my insane speed at the start. How can I be *this* tired, and my knee suddenly *this* painful, and still not have reached half way?

Paul comes through for me. He talks and talks and talks... and talks. I've since learned that this is actually his default position, talking a lot and running a lot, frequently at the same time. But with Paul yapping away beside me, pointing out people he knows, stopping for the odd photo with friends or members of his family, and regaling me with stories about his passion for running, I find I don't have to do much thinking as the miles slowly tick by.

I discover that Paul is a fanatical runner. On New Year's Day 2007, he decided to go for a run. He did the same on January 2nd. And January 3rd. And then again on the 4th, 5th, 6th... Before long, he realised it had been ages since he *hadn't* run on any given day, so he decided to try to fill the whole of 2007 with 365 runs, and not let a calendar day tick by without adding at least one run to his diary. So he did. He simply ran every day. Every single day, through rain, wind, sun, snow, illness and injury. He established a labyrinthine set of rules for himself, but basically (1) every run had to be outside, and (2) every run had to last at least 15 minutes. He's now become famous in north-east England running circles as Lord of the Streak, he's raised thousands of pounds for charity and can often be seen volunteering at local running events.

'I wasn't particularly keen on running at school. I played football, cricket, but running, take it or leave it. Then at work, some people used to run and one day I just joined in. There was a sports centre nearby, which was handy for the changing and showering, so I just started going out for runs at lunchtime. That hasn't changed now in fact, I'll still slot in my runs at lunchtime, or I'll run to work, or back home – it's amazing how you can fit your running into your working day. A lot of people use lack of time as an excuse but there's 24 hours in a day, you can always get a run in.

'But running has been particularly intense for me since 2007 when I started my streak. I'm strongly influenced by Dr Ron Hill. He's a three times Olympian turned clothing maker and is the doctor of run streak. So I just copied him kept going, every day, kept running, until... well I recently celebrated my 3,000th consecutive day by running 30 miles around a football pitch centre circle (848 laps) dressed as Bobby Moore to raise money for two charities.

'I've got a big spreadsheet with all my runs on it and I religiously keep that up to date. Because it's all about the numbers. People's birthdays. Quirky numbers. In 2012, Olympic year, I ran exactly 2,012 miles. And on 20th December that year, at 12 minutes past eight in the evening - twenty twelve on twenty twelve, Twenty Twelve - I went out and I ran 20.12 miles. It was a filthy night too, rain, wind, roads flooded, but still.'

As he's telling me this, I think about my knee and feel a little embarrassed to have made such a big deal about it at the start line. 'Don't you ever get injured?' I ask. Paul brushes off the question, a hand gesture suggesting he'd rather we change the subject. I didn't understand that gesture at the time, but I do now. We obsessive runners are always slightly injured, and we prefer not to dwell on the fact. Because yes, if we stop to think about it, it *is* a worry what we're doing, in the long term, to our feet, ankles, knees and hips. And we do notice those occasional newspaper articles suggesting that we could be doing ourselves more harm than good. If we really paused to consider it all too closely, we might think twice before heading out on that next run.

'I do get injured to be honest. But you just carry on. And people ask me if I'm ever going to stop. But why should I? It's what I do, I run every day. I'm called Lord of the Streak, not Lord of the Non-Streak. Some people read. Some people knit. Some people smoke and drink every day. Running is what I do. Stopping would do my head in.

'It's more than just ploughing out the miles. I keep it fresh. And with Facebook and Twitter (@lordsmythe), I get messages from people. And it's nice if I'm inspiring people by what I'm doing, or putting a smile on their faces with some of the costumes I've created. Sometimes I feel a little humbled by it.'

The first glimpse of the sea on Prince Edward Road in South Shields is not especially remarkable in itself, but it's brought joy to the hearts of a great many people. Because every year since 1981, Great North Runners young and old, experienced and inept, well over a million of them in total, have been greeted by that sight, and have known as they see it that months of training are almost certainly going to pay off, that there's just a mile left to go. It's where the crowds get even louder, where the finishing line first seems like a reality, and it's where, after five or so miles of mild but steady climbing, the road veers steeply downhill to give numerous, extremely tired legs a welcome respite.

'Just let your legs go, relax the muscles, you'll be amazed how fast you go with minimal effort,' says Paul at the top of the hill. I do as I'm told, and he's right. To this day I remember those words whenever I'm out on a run at the top of a sharp downhill stretch. For the first time all day, I find myself overtaking people, and find I quite like the sensation. A left turn, and the finishing line comes into view. I'm finally feeling pretty good about life, until Paul points out a grey-haired man in a bright yellow vest a little way ahead of us. Apparently he's a well-known local runner who's still going strong in his seventies.

'See if you can beat him!'

I grit my teeth. Damn right I'm going to beat some bloke more than double my age, I think, local legend or not. I force my legs to go quicker. The '800m To Go' sign is meant, I think, to give runners encouragement. But suddenly 800m seems like an awfully long way, especially with an infuriatingly speedy septuagenarian to overtake. With 400m to go, straining every sinew, I manage to inch past him and realise he's completely oblivious to the fact that anyone's even competing with him. He's simply smiling, waving, soaking up the atmosphere, enjoying what for him is the annual tradition of completing the Great North Run.

Well, sod him. One last burst of energy, using up the final dregs of fuel in the tank, and I know I've got him beat. Paul steers me over to the left of the finish area where we cross the line, blessed relief, and suddenly I'm on camera being asked how it was.

'Bloody brilliant!' I answer truthfully.

Because even though I was slower than I'd have liked (around 1:45), even though my brother-in-law beat me by miles, even though my knee hurt throughout and for most of the race I wondered how I could possibly carry on as far as the finish, the truth is – I was hooked. What a magical way to spend a Sunday morning.

Nicky Campbell

Radio and TV presenter, and a keen runner. We ran together in the hills above Rustenburg during the 2010 World Cup. He's quite quick, and looks like Forest Gump.

It's conceivable that Tom Hanks based Forest Gump's running style on me. Many years ago I was living in Hampstead in North London, and I was running at the top of Highgate Hill past some beautiful Georgian houses. I saw a guy in the entrance of a house and I thought, he looks like Tom Hanks, then I realised *he is Tom Hanks*. I ran past and looked back, and he'd come right out onto the pavement and was staring at me, staring at my style of running. I can't quite work out the timings here, it was either just before or just after the film. When it was out, I'd be running in the park and kids would point at me, barrack me, basically, saying 'That's Forrest Gump!' So either it was before the film and Tom Hanks did base Forest Gump on me – or he thought I was deliberately taking the mickey, that I'd noticed it was him and started running like Forest Gump!

I first ran in the first year of school. Every year they had a big race, about four or five miles, round the parks and the roads near the school, and everyone had to go in for it. The first time, running with the whole first year and second year, I remember emerging towards the finishing line, off the road and into a field, and I was fourth out of everybody. And because I realised I was good at it, I started really enjoying running.

I did my first marathon in 2000. It was 3:20, and I decided I wanted to try to beat three hours. So I was training, and training, and running sixty or seventy miles a week. And one day I was in Scotland, running down a hill, I pushed it too far and I knackered my knee. I had to have an arthroscopy and it's never been the same since. When the physio told me there was no way I was going to make the marathon, it felt like I was missing out on the Champions League final. I was just gutted.

But I love it. And I'm still doing it. I can still do six miles in 46 and a half, 47 minutes which is not bad at 54. I still try and run three or four times a week. It just makes me feel better. It opens my mind and I do a lot of creative stuff, writing, music, film editing… and if I'm stuck on a problem I go for a run, come back, and I've solved the problem. I've written loads of articles when I've been running. I've written them in my head and then rushed home and put them down. It's also the best way to stop feeling tired, the best way to give yourself a bit of va-va-voom.

I love running with my dog now, Maxwell. We run on a Saturday and Sunday afternoon, we do six miles together. And a bit of ball work (he chucks the ball, I run for it!), we come back, I have a cup of coffee, he lies beside me and you know… that's among my happiest moments.

And running in the Western Highlands with him, on beaches, and up mountain tracks. Every New Year I do a 12 and a half mile run on New Year's Day. Spectacular run. It's winter and you can see deer and otters and it's fantastic. So I arrive back at our gate, have a shower and a couple of Nurofen, a cup of coffee and we go over to friends and have a massive haggis lunch. And do you know what, I've earned that lunch – and my beer, and my whiskey...

◉ Pink Floyd, *Run Like Hell*

'OUTLAW' iRONMAN TRiATHLON, MiLE 6

I'm bleeding copiously, but I still feel like I'm winning. The trauma of my meteoric compulsion for the loo is fresh in my mind (although 'fresh' is the wrong word here, obviously) and I'm still buoyed by the fact I found a makeshift toilet in time. That the thorn bush appears to have done more damage than I thought is neither here nor there. It is, they are, literally just flesh wounds. And to be completely straight with you, I'm quite glad of the blood. It's a glaring, indisputable sign that I'm wounded, and a palpable focus for sympathy. I'm Bruce Willis in *Die Hard*. Only skinnier. And sweatier.

It's mile six, I'm still in pain and I'm now bleeding. But remarkably, I'm quite content as I stagger past the cricket ground at Trent Bridge. For the first time since beginning the run, the beguiling thought occurs: I might actually complete this.

'I don't think I'll complete this,' I say to my cousin.

We're on the start line of my first-ever marathon, and his fifth, in Barcelona. For me, training has been less than ideal, sprinkled with your typical novice injuries, and I've failed to complete any run longer than around 16 miles (though it's a little hard to be accurate as I measure my runs by time, not distance; my longest attempt was – checks exhaustive list of runs – two hours and seven minutes a fortnight before the marathon, after which my ankle apparently hurt so much I could barely stand up).

Following the Great North Run, in the glorious aftermath of all that positive energy on the start line, the good wishes of the crowds along the way, and the euphoria of having completed it, I was naturally keen to test myself over double the distance. The big one. An actual marathon.

I remembered when I had first decided to try to get in shape and my producer pal and I goaded each other during a crisp-fuelled break between sports bulletins, this was the holy grail we discussed, the iconic distance. The marathon was first run in Ancient Greece by a chap called Pheidippides. In about 500BC he legged it all the way from Marathon to Athens to deliver news of a military victory against the Persians. That's why marathons are called marathons. Robert Browning gave a version of the story in his poem *Pheidippides*:

> *So, when Persia was dust, all cried, 'To Acropolis!*
> *Run, Pheidippides, one race more! the meed is thy due!*
> *"Athens is saved, thank Pan," go shout!' He flung down his shield*
> *Ran like fire once more: and the space 'twixt the fennel-field*
> *And Athens was stubble again, a field which a fire runs through,*
> *Till in he broke: 'Rejoice, we conquer!' Like wine through clay,*
> *Joy in his blood bursting his heart, he died – the bliss!*

They say everybody has a marathon in them, and the fact that I'm Greek like Pheidippides definitely added to the allure. And since successfully completing 13.1 miles in South Shields, I'd been desperate to follow in the footsteps of a well-nigh national hero. But still – 26.2 miles. Such a dauntingly long way. And best not to dwell on what happened to poor old Pheidippides once he'd passed on his victorious news. Because as Browning alludes to, in quite cavalier fashion, in his poem, 'conquer' was actually the final word to pass Pheidippides' (presumably parched) lips. Here was a professional messenger, used to running long distances, but this time the mileage simply did for him. This is the match report from the Roman poet Lucian:

> *'Joy, we win!' he said, and died upon his message, breathing his last*
> *in the word 'Joy'.*

Well, I suppose you've got to hand it to Pheidippides: it's a terrific tale, his final words were memorable and his legacy is right up there. But if it's all the same to you, I'd swap all of the above for the simple pleasure of surviving my first marathon. Two and a half thousand years later, in the words of the London Marathon founder Chris Brasher, 26.2 miles has become *'the great suburban Everest'*.

After the Great North Run, riding the crest of a wave of optimism and, as Pheidippides himself said, 'joy', I did have ambitions to replicate his exact route for my debut over the distance. So I blithely entered something called the Athens Classic Marathon. It follows precisely in those ancient footsteps from Marathon to the centre of Athens, and the plan was to make the race part of a pleasant weekend away with my cousin (also called Vassos). Visit family, have some beers, run 26 miles. What could be better?

However, having paid the registration fee and booked the flights and hotel, my knee essentially imploded and I was forced to withdraw. My cousin went anyway, ran anyway, and was somewhat shocked to discover that the course is uphill, constantly, all the way from mile 6 to 21. Extraordinary finish though, in the inspirational Panathenaic Stadium. It's reconstructed from the remains of an ancient sporting arena, and it's the only stadium in the world built entirely out of marble. One of the oldest too, and certainly one of the most beautiful. It hosted the first modern Olympics of 1896, and was again involved in the Games of 2004. It's an absolute must-see on any trip to the Greek capital, probably second only to the Acropolis. I imagine a valedictory, victory lap of the Panathenaic Stadium at the end of a marathon, and you'll forgive any amount of climbing to get you there.

But apparently not. Cousin Vassos was furious about the damage the gradient had done to his finishing time, obliterating any hopes of a personal best, and he was keen to put it right as soon as possible. Having been bitten by the bug of foreign, big city marathons, he scanned the European schedule and chanced upon Barcelona. I absolutely promised to make the trip this time, though we were both busy on the Friday evening so our weekend had to be streamlined. The plan was to fly to Spain the afternoon before the race, have dinner, sleep, run, shower, and fly straight home.

I chose the hotel, the same one I'd stayed in the previous summer whilst hosting live coverage of the European Athletics Championships. It was only when we arrived that I remembered how small and difficult to sleep in the beds were, and also that most of our athletics team in Barcelona, both radio and TV, had had their credit cards cloned. So my cousin and I were careful to take our valuables with us as we headed into the city centre to find somewhere for a simple, pre-race supper. The restaurant we wandered into was warm, welcoming, weird, wonderful – but anything but simple. Portions were huge, all of them strange Catalan concoctions involving oil, onions, pork and (on two separate occasions) snails.

One of the hard and fast rules of marathon running is not to eat anything you've never tried before on the night before a big race, just in case your stomach has trouble digesting it and it adversely affects your performance the next day. You don't want to run 26.2 miles with a dicky tummy.

Well in our case, on the night before the big race, we didn't actually eat anything we *had* tried before. The supper we enjoyed that night was strange, rich, enormous and delicious. We enjoyed the meal so much, it founded a tradition – since then, every time my cousin and I have travelled abroad for a marathon (which we've done a lot), the evening before the race we find the most eclectic local restaurant we can and gorge ourselves on huge quantities of food, the more bizarre the better. We know that one day we might live to regret it – but we haven't yet. And more to the point, we don't particularly care; these suppers are outlandish, outrageous – and the risk only adds to the enjoyment.

Sleep proved problematic that night in Barcelona. Nothing to do with the meal; partly to do with the bed; and mostly to do with nerves. Maranoia, they call it. By any standards, the amount of training I'd completed was inadequate. Plus I was worrying about all my aches, pains and various injuries. If only I'd known it at the time that many of the problems I'd been complaining about were directly down to taper fever – that strange, hypochondriacal madness that affects most marathon runners, and drives their friends and family round the bend. On one occasion shortly before Barcelona, I remember being unable to walk without limping during a family weekend in Bath, and being so cross and irritable about it that even my son, then aged four, told me off for spoiling the holiday.

If I'd known that I was merely being a hypochondriac, perhaps I'd have slept in that tiny Barcelona bed. And perhaps I wouldn't have been so racked with anxiety on the start line. I genuinely believed as I lined up to begin my first marathon that I would be forced to pull out at some point before the finishing line. Then, with one minute to go until the start, I'm hit with a tremendous urge to wee. This I do recognise as psychosomatic, and before I have time to add this new issue to my exhaustive list of worries, all of a sudden we're under way.

I've installed myself in the group aiming to finish in around 3:30, and for the first few kilometres I simply enjoy the fact that I'm not being constantly overtaken. The atmosphere on the streets as we run towards and then around the famous Camp Nou, home to Barcelona FC, is a little more subdued than it was in the north east of England. I say a *little* more subdued: actually there's hardly anyone there – it's early on Sunday morning and Catalans apparently prefer to stay at home and sleep than join in what can be – if it's organised right – a mass party. There are a few, small pockets of people dotted thinly along the route – but they seem to look at us runners with a mixture of pity (*why would you want to do that?*) and irritation (*it's your fault they've closed the roads*).

For me, everything goes smoothly for the first 29km (or if you prefer, as I do, 18 miles – though of course here in Spain all the markers are in kilometres). I pass that point, realise I have just 13km (8 miles) left to run, and marvel at how comfortable it all feels. But at that very moment, someone directly in front of me pulls up and stops running, flamboyantly clutching his right hamstring and hobbling ostentatiously to the side of the road.

Something inside me breaks. I spend one second feeling real sympathy for a man who's completed 70% of a marathon only to have to pull out, another debating whether to stop and help, and a third secretly smirking at the extravagant manner of his withdrawal, comparing it to a Fernando Torres dive for a penalty. But from then on, those seconds just seem to grow longer and longer. Every one feels like a minute, and every minute like an hour as my lack of training catches up with me.

As I've mentioned, I'm not an especially quick runner, though these days I can complete a marathon in well under three hours if you ask politely. Neither am I particularly elegant. And despite the fact that I like to think I'm enjoying myself, it turns out I don't smile much when I run. So, I'm slow, ungainly and grumpy. But I do pride myself on one thing, which is this: if the question is *Can you keep going?* my answer, every time and without fail, is a resounding *Yes*.

I learn that about myself over the following 13 painful, picturesque kilometres in Barcelona. As you pass the 29km marker, the marathon route takes you south towards the sea, away from the gherkin-like Torre Agbar. That's where Fernando theatrically strains his hamstring and where I really start to slow down. However hard I try to persuade my legs to move faster, they simply refuse to.

So I dig in, and access a survival mode I never knew I possessed. Just keep going. The trick is not to look too far ahead, or the task seems too daunting. Forget the finishing line, simply try to complete twenty more paces, however painful or laboured they may be. And then, once you've done that, twenty more. Or get to the next lamppost. And then the next. To the next kilometre post. And then the next. Just keep going.

At 30km we reach the coast and turn sharp right past the triangular Fórum. I seem to be going so slowly as to be hardly moving forwards. People are streaming past me. Spirits are low. 12km on legs that feel like over-ripe bananas? Surely impossible. But if I'm going to have to give up, it's not going to be right now. Just keep going.

Every footstep of the long run by the seaside feels like an event. But I determinedly continue running, on past the Olympic Port, my legs still wailing 'stop!' as they turn right, away from the sea and out of the headwind, up past the zoological gardens towards and, fleeting thrill, through the Arc de Triomf. Still more than 5km left, still can't imagine finishing, but still refusing to stop, still continuing on, now through the Plaça de Catalunya and agonisingly catching sight of my hotel on the other side of the road and knowing that all of the pain, all of it, can end right there if I simply obey my legs and stop running. Knowing that I could be lying in a warm bath with a cold beer within minutes if I wanted to, and wanting to very badly, and most tempting of all knowing that nobody would really care if I did decide to quit right here...

Nobody, that is, except me.

So I wrench my gaze away from the open lobby doorway and renew my resolve to *just keep going*. On past the Picasso Museum, past the cathedral, and suddenly past a marker saying 40km, and dimly grasping the fact that I'm close enough now to sense for the first time that I might actually finish this thing. I realise I would *crawl* the remaining 2.2km if needs be. I am about to join the marathon club. I am about to become Pheidippides.

Newly energised, I decide to see how fast (or slowly) I'm actually running. I make a mental note of the time on my stopwatch as I pass 40km, and shuffle onwards to the next distance marker. But it doesn't exist. However far I run, the 41km post simply isn't there. I start to believe that I must have missed it, either that or they don't bother with markers so close to the finish. But just then the number 41 looms into view appallingly far ahead. Eventually I reach it and look again at my watch. It's taken me over six minutes to travel one kilometre.

Another loud thud of realisation inside my head: if I don't get a move on, I won't break four hours. I get a move on. I'm drawn towards the distant sound of cheering in what has now become a crowded start/finish area, soon I can also hear an excitable Spanish commentator jibber-jabbering on the tannoy, then I see the red roof of the inflatable arch that I ran through at the start early this morning, and before I know it, after almost four hours of constant running, I'm back underneath it and crossing the finishing line.

I've just completed my first marathon.

I frequently hear people in the same situation categorically say 'never again'. Well if you'd told me at that moment that this marathon would be the first of many, that I would spend the next few years allowing long-distance running to define me in many respects, I honestly would have been thrilled.

Don't tell Pheidippides, but finishing a marathon gives you a sumptuous sense of achievement.

Angi Copson

Only started running aged 59, but has since won many age group titles and set many world records, including in the 1500m, 3000m and 5000m Over-65 category. Her marathon world record is a staggering 3 hours and 17 minutes.

People often ask me why I started running late in life. I felt a little bit embarrassed when I started to run, I live in a small village and everyone knows what you are doing. They know exactly when you go out and exactly when you come back. It seemed strange to them all to see a 60-year-old woman going out running and even my family thought I was a little bit crazy. Sometimes I'd even run at night so no one could see me! I guess I'm still the only one around here my age that goes out and runs but now it's getting better and better because age doesn't seem to matter; anyone can pick up a pair of trainers and give it a go.

My father died of cancer when I was young, so my sisters and I were raised by my mother alone. When I started school I was such a sickly child I was never encouraged to do sport, which probably would have done me good, but years ago it was all so different. By the time I was doing my own thing I had a love for horse riding, and when my son and daughter came along they had a pony, so running was never thought of. But then a few years back my husband Harry had to have heart surgery. Afterwards he was told to do more exercise so he bought a bike and I would jog along with him to keep him company.

In 2006 we went to the London Marathon to support my friend's daughter. The atmosphere was amazing and suddenly I knew I wanted to be part of the 2007 Marathon. Eventually I got a place with Heart Research. I had just six months to get fit and raise lots of money! My first run was just along to the next village and back. I was absolutely exhausted by the time I had done one mile and probably only ran two miles that day and then three miles the next. It's slow when you start running and aren't too fit but I stuck with it over the next months.

22 April 2007 was one of the hottest ever days for the London Marathon. It was also one day after my 60th birthday; running under four hours and raising £3,500 was the best birthday present ever!

After the marathon, encouraged by a friend of mine, I joined Rugby and Northampton Running Club. I loved the club competitions, and it was a new experience training with others. There was a great mix of people, all young, active and laughing. I'm still keeping up with them each Sunday on a long run, which is good. I know when the time comes and I can't stay with the pace, they won't just ditch me, they'll run on and run back to me – that's the type of people they are. Running with them gave me strength and confidence.

In 2008 I was back to run London again in 3 hours 15 minutes, which gave me a place on the elite start in 2009. The competitions and races are great; 2012 was an amazing year for me, as I was thrilled to be awarded the European Masters Woman Athlete of the Year.

I love running with other people but I also enjoy running on my own. You can actually put things together when you're on your own. You don't feel unsociable. I love my thinking and sorting out, and probably next week's menu is done on my runs on my own.

Since I have become a runner I am a much stronger person in many ways. I have three grandchildren, two of them still toddlers and they are very active to be with, probably the next runners in our family.

Recently I came across an old photo of my grandfather, dressed in running kit, standing by a table full of trophies; I must have got the genes from him.

Running has turned my life around and I have met some great people as well as great athletes. If you're thinking of running, don't be worried; just go slow, take it slow. Whatever your age, you can run.

◉ Paul McCartney, *Band on the Run*

'OUTLAW' iRONMAN TRiATHLON, MiLE 7

Right then, time to focus on my right calf.

I've been concerned since the start of the bike ride that it might not get me through to the finish line. But perhaps I should be worrying more long term. The ache from this morning has become a searing pain, and I'm fairly sure that I'm doing the poor muscle some lasting damage by carrying on regardless. I'm no stranger to injuries, and still wince when I remember the two extended, enforced breaks from running I was forced to endure with dodgy knees. These harrowing run-free periods were both before I learned to improve my gait, but as I hobble into mile seven, I begin to contemplate a short- to medium-term future without running in it. Doesn't bear thinking about.

Equally unpalatable is the prospect of having to give up my cycle commute. I treasure the 30 pre-dawn minutes alone on the bike on the way to Radio 2. Gets the heart going, wakes me up (crucially), gives me time to think and generally sets me up for the day. But given that the calf started hurting today while I was in the saddle, I begin to consider that I may well have to give my trusty bike a rest too. What a horrible prospect – starting every day pushing an ignition button, not down on a pedal. Long weeks without my BFG (stands for Big Friendly Giant – my kids named the now slightly shabby utility bike, a Giant Rapid, when she was all white and shiny and new, and the name has sort of stuck in my head).

So at this rate, I'll simply be swimming for the rest of the summer. Nothing against swimming – it's the big revelation of this triathlon, how much I've enjoyed my swimming. But indoors every day? Up and down the same 20m pool in my local gym? Up and down... Up, turn. Back, turn... No running, no cycling, no enjoying the sunshine. And not just for a week. For months on end potentially... Up, turn... Back, turn... All. Summer. Long.

Put it like that, and I should definitely stop. There'd be absolutely no disgrace in simply slowing down to a walk (there wouldn't be much slowing down involved) and retiring hurt. People have been dropping out all over the place, especially in this heat. And this is a proper, grown-up muscle injury we're talking about.

So should I stop now? Obviously, yes I should. Unquestionably. Undeniably.

Will I stop? Not a chance in hell. Just keep going.

Scott Mitchell has the calming, efficient air of someone who's seen it all before. On the day I first met him, he welcomed me affably into his physiotherapy clinic, and listened with a warm smile as I outlined my symptoms – I had what I described as a hurty knee. This gentle, slender Australian was about to inflict all manner of agony upon me, but to look at him you'd never have known it. The problem turned out to be ITBS, Iliotibial Band Syndrome, or just plain old Runner's Knee. It's a classic novice's injury.

By this time, I'd been running for a few months, and was starting to enjoy it. Starting to experiment a little too. How far could I go? How fast could I go? And could I keep running even though the outside of my left knee had just started hurting?

The answer to this last question, surprisingly, was yes. When it first strikes, ITBS tends to start aching around five minutes into a run, a mildly grating, gnawing sort of pain which hangs around for a while without really seeming to be doing much damage, then disappears for the rest of the run, only to reappear again five minutes into tomorrow's run.

So I of course, had made the classic beginner's error and ignored the pain until my knee was hurting permanently. Only then did I belatedly seek medical attention, and lucked out with my choice of physio.

'The issue is not your knee,' he told me, and explained that the problem lay with something called an iliotibial band which, I learned, is the ligament that runs down the outside of the thigh from the hip and attaches to the knee. And even though it was my knee that hurt, the source was further up the leg in my glutes. Which, I further discovered, is physio-speak for 'bottom'.

I lay on my front and prepared to be made better. I was actually quite looking forward to it, expecting a kind of medical massage. What happened next made me jump off the table in agony.

Scott started to try and unknot some especially tight muscles in my bum (gluteal trigger points, he called them) and basically elbowed me hard in the outside of the hip. It felt like he'd just electrocuted my skeleton. He persuaded me to man up and lie back down. The rest of the hour was spent with me screwing up my face against what felt like bright red pain whilst Scott calmly and casually continued with his elbow torture like some kind of sadistic antipodean Bond villain.

But the thing is, it worked. I can't think of many examples of 'good pain' but this definitely counts. Usually when you're hurting, it's your body's way of telling you that something's not right. But this elbow-induced agony made me feel generally looser from the hips down and miraculously removed the cause of the Runner's Knee (though Mike from The Running School would doubtless tell you that the *actual* cause was a flaw in my technique). I also learned that it can be a good idea to use a foam roller or sit on a tennis ball from time to time – if it hurts, it's doing you good. Painful, but beneficial-painful. Like the week-long headache I'm told comes on when you give up caffeine, though quite honestly I'm unlikely to ever find that one out.

Anyway, going to a physio was a revelation, and allowed me to take my running up a few gears. I did become a bit of a regular in Scott's clinic but his expert diagnosis helped me through pretty much all of my first half-dozen marathons.

In the first few years of running, as well as the Runner's Knee, I managed to stockpile quite a collection of injuries. Before my unwieldy octopus-gait was fixed, I picked up shin splints, the odd hamstring strain, an achy Achilles and several variations on the hurty knee theme. Dr Internet, I found, was generally terrible at diagnosing my injuries, so mostly I went to Scott – and mostly he made it better. On the eve of one marathon, almost unable to walk without pain, he put strapping all over my lower leg to hold the muscles and joints in place and remarkably it worked (I'd had my doubts). I got through 26.2 miles without making anything worse – and was OK to resume running within days.

Occasionally, however, he'd advise me to take a complete rest from running, which of course was my least favourite course of treatment, and advice I sometimes chose to ignore. But it's amazing how quickly a small problem can become a big problem if you continue running on it. And it's equally amazing how quickly the body can cure itself when it's not under continual stress. Whenever I followed Scott's recommendations, I'd almost always be back on the roads within a week.

Mind you, those weeks did feel like months whilst in the thick of them. Cross-training in the gym, swimming, rowing on the ergo, even cycling – for me, all are satisfying supplements to running, but poor substitutes. If the running bug bites as hard as it did me, you do pretty much anything to avoid prolonged periods without lacing up your trainers.

Eccentric exercises for instance. (That's not eccentric meaning odd, but eccentric the opposite of concentric, the working muscle lengthening rather than shortening.) Recovery from one recurrent pain in the front of my knee involved going to the gym every other day, somehow manufacturing a downslope of about 30 degrees using two perpendicular exercise steppers and slowly lowering myself on alternate legs for half an hour. Come to think of it, perhaps the exercises were both eccentric (opposite of concentric) and eccentric (odd) – certainly if the looks I received from the other gym users were anything to go by.

I've also taken it upon myself to try core-strengthening exercises of every conceivable description and difficulty. I've worked on my posture.

I've tried to correct an instinctive, constant lean to the left, borne of being blind in one eye. And I've instigated several regimes of varying lunacy to try to improve my stability – once, every evening for a month, I cleaned my teeth standing on one leg with my eyes closed. All in a bid to lessen the chances of sustaining a running injury, and having to take time off.

Only twice have I seriously doubted Scott's diagnosis. Both times wrongly as it happens, but both times I simply didn't like what I was hearing and went to a sports doctor for a second opinion. Because I was hearing from Scott that I would have to stop running for weeks, maybe months. And by then, that was unthinkable.

Sally Gunnell OBE

Olympic, World, European and Commonwealth 400m hurdles champion, and world record holder. The only female British athlete to have achieved that feat.

The day I first realised that I could run fast, I was still very young, still at primary school. We were playing kiss chase in the school playground. There was some boy that I didn't really fancy and I found I could run away from him. I just really remember thinking 'wow, I'm quite fast'.

Meanwhile, probably around the same sort of age, there was my first experience of sports day. I won this bright orange bowl and I remember so vividly running down the straight and thinking 'wow, I've won!' And it was such a lovely feeling to feel free and be doing something that you loved and were actually good at. I don't think there was much else that I was good at, at that age.

When I was around 12, I joined a club and in fact I started off as a long jumper. It was okay. Then it was heptathlon, and again I was all right at it. After that came the 100m hurdles, and I was bit better still... It took me a long time to find what I really was good at, what I was going to excel at. But all through those early days, I just loved being part of the club. I enjoyed getting on the bus at the weekend, going to an athletics meet.

I loved the banter on the bus and my best friends were on that bus. I met them all through the running club.

It was a completely social thing – and in fact I would say that a lot of my career was based around relishing the social side of it. Yes, of course I also wanted to be the best that I could be and I wanted to see how fast I could run. And I guess it got serious towards the end, but there was always the simple love of it. I appreciated that feeling of understanding yourself as a person.

When I'm actually running, when I'm out there and I'm in full flight, I love the thinking time that it allows me. I mean, don't get me wrong, there are days when I run and I really don't want to be doing it, but the bit I still love is the feeling afterwards. So there might be days where I think I should really go out for a half-hour run now, and even though I can't be bothered I still do, and that feeling when I finish – that is why I do it.

And then there's that satisfaction when you think 'yeah, I've done some exercise today and now I can eat cake!'

◉ Snow Patrol, *Run*

'OUTLAW' iRONMAN TRiATHLON, MiLE 8

I'm over-thinking this. With every step, the only thing that crosses my mind is how much I'm dreading the next step, and the 50,000 after that. Which, incidentally, is one of the pieces of information I wish I could unlearn – that a marathon is around 50,000 footsteps. It's not something I tend to think about as I go about my day-to-day life, but put me on a marathon start line and within the first mile, that QI fact will pop unbidden into my head, and do its best to sabotage my spirits. Today more than ever. Fifty. Thousand. Steps.

I try to work out approximately how many of the 50,000 I have left. The answer is just under 35,000, which is fairly simple mental arithmetic but it takes an agreeably disproportionate amount of time to work out. Anyone who's ever run so much as a 10k knows how slowly the brain works when the body's under duress. That, and I can't multi-task at the best of times. So I've found that trying to solve a mathematical conundrum is a terrific way of *not* focusing on just how long a long run is. Indeed it takes much of mile eight just to realise that, forget the footsteps, I now have fewer than twenty miles left to run.

Whenever that thought occurs mid-marathon, it's always accompanied by a stab of happiness. However, it's followed today by another mental intruder in the form of an old running truism, 'If you reach mile 20 of a marathon and you're struggling, that's normal. If you reach half way and you're struggling, you're in trouble. And if you're struggling with 20 miles to go, you're for it.'

Well, I was struggling with the entire marathon ahead of me. Worse, I began struggling with 100 miles to go on the bike. In fact the last time I *wasn't* struggling, I still had wet hair from the swim.

Prognosis: alarming.

A Sunday morning alone at home with the children. Unfortunate that it coincides with one of the increasingly rare instances when I wake up in a blind panic. Nothing I can do to stop them. During my teens and twenties it would happen quite frequently, and I'd simply swallow down the darkness and force myself into the day. I'm thankful it's now once in a blue moon, but it still feels pretty rotten when it strikes. Like I'm already losing before the day has even started. Everybody has their gremlins, and these are mine. I don't think I'm particularly unusual, but the gremlins do need putting back in their box. People try loads of different things, some go to psychotherapists, others suffer from anger or addiction. But in my humble opinion, the quickest, surest, easiest way to improve your sense of self-worth is to go for a run.

Just starting out on the road to fitness automatically makes you feel better about yourself. Impossible not to, when you're doing yourself some good, doing yourself a favour. And of all the fitness recipes available, I'm convinced that running has the edge. Running outside, that is.

Here's why.

If you're in the gym, whatever you're doing, whether you're on a cross-trainer, or rowing, stepping, static cycling, weight training, even on the treadmill, you're involved in a machine, or a thing, which inherently draws your focus. Part of you is concentrating on how long is left, how fast you're going, how many calories you're burning, how many reps, how many revs and so on. Your subconscious mind is much less free to do its thing. Plus, crucially, you're indoors – there are walls, which act like mental barriers. Swimming in a pool has much the same effect: your mind has little time to wander before you reach the side and have to start over. Cycling outside, if you're *not* concentrating on the cars, you're in trouble.

And what about team sports? Well, yes, fantastic – indeed I'm such a fan, I've spent half a lifetime paying to watch them and the other half being paid to. And it doesn't have to be the top-level stuff. I've also been lucky enough to see at first hand how team sports can transform the lives of underprivileged kids: they're wonderful moments these, watching disadvantaged young people unite into a cohesive team. As Sir Keith Mills, who helped stage the London Olympics and Paralympics and now runs the charity Sported, said to me just before we went live on air for an interview: 'Sport is just brilliant!' This was on the first morning of the first-ever Invictus Games (a sporting event for wounded, injured and sick Servicemen and women), and never did his words feel more appropriate. Sport *is* just brilliant. Team sports will get you fit and give you a sense of belonging and purpose. Same with the gym and same with swimming lengths. Brilliant. Just brilliant.

But the thing with running outside, the real added value and USP, is that it does all of the above whilst also giving you thinking space. And frequently, your conscious mind isn't even the part of your brain doing the thinking – you don't even know it's happening. Your brain could be filled with the music that's playing in your earphones, or enjoying the scenery, looking forward to a night out, or complaining that the blister on your left foot has begun to hurt again despite those expensive plasters you bought... anything really. Meantime, your subconscious mind seems to reset itself, to perform a mid-exercise ctrl-alt-del, and whether you're aware it's happening or not, when you've finished your run, you simply feel better about life. Other exercise does the same job, running outside just does it better.

So on that Sunday morning when I woke up in a panic, my first priority was to get myself outside and running. Didn't matter that it was the last thing I felt like doing, didn't matter that it was raining and I had the kids in tow. I simply bribed them onto their bikes, laced up my trainers, braved the elements, and got out there.

And of course it worked, as I knew it would. A terrible morning in prospect became really rather lovely. It was just another rainy weekend and we didn't do anything unusual, but I remember the day because it was the first time I felt acutely grateful for having discovered running. Exhilarated by our rain-sodden early exercise, we joyfully dried ourselves off whilst enjoying the marshmallows in hot chocolate I'd used earlier as a bribe. We unsuccessfully attempted to bake a healthy cake, we built silly things with Lego, played a board game, went to the pub for lunch, all of us happy, all of us light-hearted, all of us laughing – and all because of a 30-minute easy run round an unknowing bend in the River Thames.

So yes. Running outdoors, especially off-road and, curious as it may seem, in bad weather, truly seems to heal the soul.

Which brings me on to the thorny issue of running in the rain. I'm really not sure how I feel about it. Do I enjoy it? Do I pretend to enjoy it? Do I force myself to enjoy it? Or actually, if I'm honest, do I kind of dislike it?

I'm writing these words on a late winter's Wednesday afternoon. I was tired a few hours ago, and debated whether to nip upstairs for a nap, or head outside in the driving rain for a run. It's the age-old question whenever you're after a quick pick-me-up: sleep or run? And the answer is simple, however difficult and counterintuitive it may seem: run, every time.

So summoning up some willpower, I decided on my favourite hour-long, eight-mile easy loop to the park and back. The dog looked unusually sceptical as we set off.

Ten minutes later, I understood why. The rain that had been heavy as we started was now at monsoon levels. By the time we were three miles and 20-odd minutes away from home, it was raining like the end of the world. In the distance, I imagined all different kinds of animals heading two by two into an enormous ark.

It was becoming difficult to see. The wind had picked up and as the water hit my face, it almost hurt. Massive raindrops were exploding onto the pavement, ominous puddles appearing by the side of the road. Almost at once a passing lorry drove through a big one right beside me.

But by now I was so wet I was beyond caring. In fact I realised I was almost delighting in how wet I was, and how little it mattered. It felt liberating to be this wet. Like Andie MacDowell at the end of *Four Weddings and a Funeral*. Hugh Grant sees her in the church and calls off his imminent wedding. Outside, it's pouring as they kiss, both of them wet through. 'Let's get out of this rain,' says Hugh. 'Is it raining?' Andie asks. 'I hadn't noticed.' And I understood exactly how she felt. I was also feeling so euphoric, I no longer noticed how soaking I was.

No question, there's a certain perverse pleasure to be running – to be choosing to be outside and running as opposed to inside and sitting – through ridiculous rainstorms. The start is nasty, uncomfortable, but you soon get used to it. Running kit sticks to the body in odd, strangely agreeable places. And the downpour adds a certain intensity to the whole experience, in the same way as it can when you're watching live football through driving rain.

Also, you feel kind of hard. And I don't get many chances. I've only been involved in three fights in my life, and of those, I only won one. It was in Lithuania in the mid-90s, and an aggressive drunk was harassing some of my university friends. He took a wild swing at me when I told him to stop, and I instinctively punched him back. And that, surprisingly, was all it took to end it. Now of course fighting's not right and kids – Emily, Matthew, Mary – if you're reading this any of you, then you should know that Daddy's not proud of punching someone. You should also know that it genuinely hurts your fist when it connects at pace with a jaw. But actually, between you and me, whisper it quietly and definitely don't tell your mother, Daddy secretly *is* proud of that night in Vilnius. Not only did he stand up for his friends, but he had the brawn to back it up when attacked.

And I undeniably look back on that incident with much fonder memories than my other two brushes with any sort of street violence – once in South Africa when I was mugged and beaten up a bit, and once in Hammersmith when some youths pulled a knife but I managed to wriggle free and run away across the bridge. They did follow for a bit, the four young men in hoodies who'd rudely demanded my wallet and phone, but it's amazing what blind panic does to your speed. If I could hire them to stand behind me on the start line of my next 5k, I would absolutely *obliterate* my PB.

Oh, and now I think about it, there was recently some argy-bargy with a fellow cyclist one evening in central London. I admonished him for stupidly going through a red light, he vehemently took exception and came back to tell me about it. But just as the verbals escalated into pushing and shoving, two things happened simultaneously which allowed us both to go our separate ways with pride intact – just barely, in my case. (1) A double decker appeared in the bus lane we were blocking and hooted impatiently for us to move, and (2) I suddenly remembered that in my haste to get home from the TV studios where I'd just been presenting a sports show, I'd forgotten to remove my make-up. So whilst Mr Redlightjumper paused to consider the bus, and I paused to consider whether anyone would have noticed in the dark that I was wearing foundation (and also whether that should matter either way), the sting was taken out of the situation and we both harrumphed our separate ways.

So basically, in forty years of enjoying a middle-class existence in one of the safest countries on earth, opportunities to feel hard have been few and far between. That's why when I was out running today in just shorts and a T-shirt and it was properly soaking and utterly freezing, I liked how it was undeniably robust and rugged.

Then of course I arrived home dripping water and mud all over the clean carpet. And as I write, the smell of wet dog has permeated the whole house, my sodden kit lies in a sad, deflated pile in the corner and it'll take days for my shoes to dry properly. And I'll probably get a cold. But then again, there's nothing quite like that post-rain, post-run shower…

All very confusing and the jury's still out on running in the rain. But I'll tell you something: I'm definitely pleased I didn't have a nap instead.

Noel Thatcher MBE

Six-time Paralympian, and five times Paralympic gold medallist. World record holder. Now a leading physiotherapist.

I was born with a visual impairment, a degenerative condition of the optic nerve and retinal cells, but up until the age of 10 I went through regular mainstream education. I had some issues at primary school and couldn't really find anything I could succeed at, but I just thought that was because I was poor at sport and uncoordinated.

When I was 10 my parents made the decision to send me to a school for the blind and visually impaired in Coventry. This was run by a headmaster who'd had extensive military experience and ran it accordingly. And as part of the 'character building' ethos of the school, he had all the boys in the four houses go out and do house runs – three times a week, summer and winter. So every other day we'd have to go out and run two or three miles, whatever the weather, and I bloody hated it. With a passion.

In fact I hated running so much I did everything in my power to get out of it. We used to do three laps of the road round the school, and I'd jump into the hedge on the first lap and only join in again for the last lap. Or I'd feign illness. Or injury. Anything! But it very rarely got me out of it, and I continued to hate running until I was 12, and that was when I fell under the influence of a mate who suggested we go off and have a mid-run fag. 'Come on,' he said, 'no one will notice.'

So we headed off to a disused railway siding where I smoked my first and only cigarette. But it took us almost 90 minutes to do a two-mile run, and the housemaster was understandably concerned when he caught up with us. He smelled our breath, realised what had happened, and the punishment he meted out was daily runs. Five miles a night for a month, with the housemaster following in his car, or hiding behind hedges, and every time we showed signs of slowing down he'd leap out and shout and scream. In fact he was a great guy, but it was an interesting model of education!

So at the end of this Kenyan-esque camp, I went back to the school cross country, and instead of finishing 86th out of 89, and walking most of the way, I came third. This was a bit of a shock to everybody, most of all me, because I never thought I had any particular gift for it. And also, as I hated the sport, I wasn't really that interested in it. But there's a lot of kudos that goes with sporting success in a boarding school. That cross country was my first real exposure to it, and I found that I kind of liked it.

Then of course when you become part of a team, you begin to develop a little more self-esteem, and that helps build confidence. As a school, we then went on to win the Warwickshire Schools Cross Country Championships, which was a huge achievement for a school of visually impaired kids who in the local community were always seen as 'special' (in the non-complimentary sense). In fact that's still one of my proudest achievements, because in those days it's something that wouldn't have even been conceived of.

At the same sort of time, we also had the triple A [Amateur Athletics Association] FiveStar awards scheme going, so during the summer you could score points for your performance in different events; they'd all be added up and you apply for different star awards badges. In our school we were sports mad, so we weren't just happy getting five star badges for our own age group: we'd then go for five stars for the age group above us. And I got sucked into that whole competitive thing where my mates and I were simply competing for competition's sake.

And the school was tremendously supportive. In fact I was still at school when I went to my first championships. It was my first year of A-Levels when we went to the European Championships in Bulgaria, which at the time was Eastern Bloc and it was my first experience of foreign travel apart from family holidays. And half the team came from the school I was at. So, away with your mates on a week-long athletics camp with all that goes with it – if I'm honest it was about eight parts holiday and two parts athletics, but it was incredible. Same with the 1984 Paralympics. There were 20 visually impaired athletes and swimmers in total, and 10 of them came from our school. The Paralympics were in New York, and we felt a little hard done by to be at a university campus on Long Island. Again though, I mostly treated it as a holiday – and just like as a 17-year-old in Budapest, I ended up with a silver medal.

On both occasions my abiding memories are of crossing the finishing line to find the winner lying flat on the ground in a pool of sweat and lactate – and realising that's what it took to win. Very quickly after that, I stopped looking at these trips simply as excellent holidays. I was lucky enough to be coached by John Anderson who also looked after David Moorcroft and Liz McColgan amongst a huge number of other very talented athletes. And gold medals were the yardstick. When I won silver in New York, I was the only person in our dorm not to be going home with a gold.

And by the time I got to Seoul in 1988, the Paralympic Games were characterised for me by huge amounts of self-inflicted pressure. I'd won the World Championships and set a new 800m world record two years previously – and in Seoul it was all about expectation, pressure, nerves... the whole nine yards.

Retrospectively, I loved running but was absolutely scared stupid of competing and failing. I learned the hard way that pressure can be a very negative force in an athlete's life. Did I enjoy competing all the time? Certainly not in Seoul. That was hellish, even though I won the 800m by four hundredths of a second having been pushed off the track with 150 metres to go. I had a borderline eating disorder leading up to that as I'd got myself so screwed up – and all because I'd convinced myself that winning the gold medal was the only thing that mattered in life.

But the love of running, that simple love of running, the thing that gets you out when it's pouring down with rain, out of bed in the mornings when there's no one else around, that never leaves you. You couldn't compete for so long – and I've been doing it for over forty years now – you couldn't do it without that innate love of running.

The competitive element blunts the enjoyment for me now. So turning up at a race and pinning a number to my chest, I'm not especially interested in that anymore (though having said that I'm about to run a competitive marathon in Japan).

These days it's about getting the most enjoyment out of every single run, whatever the circumstances and whatever the context. If it's a three-mile recovery run on a Monday morning round our local park, then I'm looking at the trees, breathing in the air and living the moment. And if it's a 20-mile tempo run, I'm still trying to get the most out of that.

As I always say, never leave a run feeling anything negative about it. With running, you can win every day.

🎵 Lenny Kravitz, *Always on the Run*

'OUTLAW' iRONMAN TRiATHLON, MiLE 9

Another troubling development. My left knee has swollen up to disturbing proportions. I'm trying not to notice this new pain, and that's actually proving relatively straightforward (though in the long term, rather worrying) because all I have to do to block out the misery in my knee is to focus instead on somewhere else that's suffering. There are several lively candidates.

There's the ongoing issue of the calf muscle. There's my lower back and middle, now feeling like an overused fold in a piece of paper, like it's going to give up the ghost any second and simply let the two halves tear away from each other. And I'm increasingly cross with my wrists for adding to the general discomfort. I mean, wrists?

Oh, and the stomach. The whole thing now feels like it's part of some grotesque, agonising washing machine spin cycle. Whilst continuing all the while to throw up nasty, noxious bile which I'm trying, and frequently failing, to swallow back down.

So yes, it's easy enough to ignore the knee if I want to. It's been problematic in the past, but never felt like this before. Clearly, a knee doesn't almost double in size without good (or should that be bad?) reason, and as it happens that knee will never be quite the same again. It still hurts most days. But to be honest by mile nine I'm beyond caring. It's got to the stage where I almost welcome the extra challenge.

Bring it on, knee.

Simon Kemp is a very good doctor. And an exceptionally good sports injury doctor. Possibly the best there is.

You want an imposing list of post-name letters? You've got them: he is Dr Simon Kemp MA MB BS MSc(SEM) MRCGP FFSEM. You want an impressive CV? Check this out: he's treated injured rugby players in New Zealand, lectured in Sports Medicine at the Queens Medical Centre, been team doctor for Fulham Football Club, medical officer to the English Basketball Association and, since 2001, head of sports medicine at the Rugby Football Union. If you're the richest national governing body of the most injury-prone sport on the planet, you make sure you're getting the finest medical advice available. Indeed we pretty much have Simon Kemp to thank for keeping Jonny Wilkinson fit enough to kick that dramatic World Cup-winning drop goal in Sydney in 2003.

He's also been at the vanguard of the RFU's recent endeavours to better understand and treat the numerous, often serious, injuries rugby players sustain, including concussion. You've probably seen him being interviewed on the news. Like I say, Simon Kemp may just be the best sports injury doctor out there. I'm lucky to see him in person in his clinic in Wimbledon. I still have a hurty knee.

It's long before the Ironman, even before the Great North Run, and I'm refusing to believe physio Scott's assertion that I should take a long break from running. Instead, I'm hoping that someone used to putting rugby players back together will have a magic bullet where an amateur runner is concerned.

Simon assesses me, interrogates me, gets me balancing on one bare foot then the other, examines, pokes, prods, asks more pertinent questions – then confirms Scott's diagnosis of severe ITBS. I had been worried about needing an operation, but Simon reassures me that's extremely unlikely. Rest and rehab will see you right, he confidently asserts. And as he prepares to welcome in the next patient (a woman apparently more injured than I am who's about to attempt a half-Ironman), he cheerfully suggests I go to see Mike at The Running School to try to stop the problem at source.

The thing that never fails to impress about Simon Kemp is his straightforward attitude to sports injury. The two issues I've been to see him about both cleared up precisely how and exactly when he said they would. He's also borderline obsessed with his own performances on a road bike, and I can relate to that too. Middle-aged bloke trying to recapture some of his lost youth by getting infatuated with his own mediocre sporting efforts and achievements? Yep!

Anyway, Simon's agreed to answer some questions and quite honestly, if you're a runner or considering becoming one – you could do a lot worse than read on.

So what's the typical injury a new runner will come to see you with?
They usually come with a lower leg overload problem that's developed because they've increased their running load (a combination of distance, frequency and speed) too quickly – greater than the recommended maximum 10% increase per week – and they don't have a background as a runner. The common running problems are all theoretically preventable. Achilles tendonopathy. Patellar tendonopathy. Patellofemoral knee pain. Gluteal tendonopathy. Hamstring tendonopathy. Or, much less commonly, lower limb stress fractures. All should be preventable with a sensible approach to planning a training programme.

So how would you prevent them?
Rather than just taking on board the standard advice, the runner needs to think about their potential risk of injury. I think it's helpful to categorise themselves into red, amber or green risk categories. Both their initial running loads and first running goal need to be proportionate to where they are starting from. And really, the approach for each of these three groups needs to be different.

Green is: I've always been a regular runner. I may have lapsed for a little while, but I ran at school and/or university, and I haven't had long periods of not running.

Amber is: I've run on and off, I've done other sports, I've remained fit and active. Maybe I've not been running that much recently but I've been doing running-related activities – football, tennis, hockey etc. regularly.

The Red group is: I don't have any significant previous regular running experience. I may be heavy. Any exercise that I've done recently has been on a bike (limited weight-bearing) or in the swimming pool. I may have had previous problems when I have run, I may know that I have knee pain, hip pain. I may have had previous lower limb surgery. I may have had a previous fracture to the leg or ankle.

Whilst the Green group might start training for a half-marathon, the Red group needs to set more realistic goals – possibly 5km or 10km rather than a half-marathon and start running less often each week, at a slower pace for less time until they develop the robustness they need to increase the amount they run. They can get there but they need to take it more slowly than the green group and allow more time for recovery between runs. They may well benefit from some non-running-based training to help them become more 'robust'.

Why have you got me standing barefoot on one leg when I've come to see you?
Running involves absorbing load with each foot strike. Think about the legs as a chain. You need to make sure that you're as stable at the contact of your foot with the ground and the junction of the leg with the pelvis as possible. In order to do that you need to be running in a shoe that makes your foot–ground contact as effective as possible. And if you have rapidly collapsing arches to your feet, if you're a marked pronator*, you may need a shoe that in some way limits that. Equally at the top end of the chain, where your thigh joins your pelvis, you need enough gluteal/lower back/abdominal stability, for your pelvis to remain stable when you are weight bearing on one leg and the other leg is swinging forwards. This stability can be developed relatively easily with specific exercises. And when I get you to stand on one leg, what I'm doing is assessing both ends. The key here is that you may need to work on both ends

---

* Pronation is the inward movement of the foot to distribute the force of impact as you run. Everybody does it, but runners who do it too much, who over-pronate, often need orthotics or motion control shoes.

of the chain and not just one end. So if you're strong in your glutes but you're in the wrong shoes, you may have a problem. And if you've got the right shoes but you've still got weak glutes, that's also often an issue.

People who have a strong core, well-conditioned glutes and legs that have been exposed to some resistance training are likely to be able to tolerate a running load better than somebody who's trained on a bike or only done irregular yoga.

But there's another accepted principle that may override all of this. There is huge variation between individuals (who appear broadly similar) in their risk of injury. In cycling people talk about macro-absorbers and micro-adjusters. The macro-absorbers can ride without problems irrespective of how the bike is set up. And there are others (the micro-adjusters) for whom a 2mm change in the seat position is enough to give them lower back pain so bad it may preclude them from cycling. The same is true for runners: if you have flat or pronating feet but those feet don't cause you any problems, then you don't need to do anything about it. You need to think about the whole person.

I thank Simon and tell him I hope to see him soon. That's not entirely truthful; I hope I *don't* see him soon in his professional capacity as that would mean another injury. And as he's keen to stress, you don't necessarily have to end up in his clinic just because you decide to start running.

You've asked me about injury and it's all too easy to stress the downside of exercise without promoting the upside. Running is a convenient, effective and accessible way to improve your health whether that is lowering your blood pressure, losing weight or reducing your risk of heart disease, diabetes, stroke or cancer. Exercise is the most effective medicine and the overall health benefits of running are overwhelmingly positive.

Jenson Button MBE

Formula One World Champion, and an exceptionally accomplished runner and triathlete. Jenson has even founded his own triathlon, the popular Jenson Button Trust Triathlon, to raise money for cancer charities.

I don't remember when I first started running. I think we were all running as kids, weren't we? I'm an eighties child so we didn't have iPhones and tablets and what have you back then, so it was outside sports all the way. I was always active but really I didn't start training or running until I got seriously into karting. When I was 14 I started racing in go-karts in Europe and also racing in Japan and America and that's when I realised I needed to be a bit fitter. In fact it came from a big push from my dad who told me how important fitness was. That got me hooked at a really early age – and I've been hooked ever since.

For me, it's so peaceful getting out and going for a run. I live in the South of France in Monaco so it's perfect to head down the coast or up into the hills. It's more of a release than anything else for me. I really enjoy my time when I'm running. There's also the fun runs round circuits of course. Every race we go to, many of the extended Formula One family, from drivers to mechanics to broadcasters, run the circuit for charity. So there are lots of people, hundreds of people sometimes, out on the circuit running for charity. And that is pretty awesome, and creates an amazing atmosphere.

Whilst I'm out on my runs I've listened to music in the past but recently I've started taking in my surroundings a bit more. I'm very lucky that I get to go to some great places with F1, so I do think it's more important to enjoy your surroundings than to listen to music. And when I was in training for the London Marathon, I really had to learn to take in my surroundings a lot, because many of the training runs were so long!

Before I ran London for the first time, I'd only ever run one marathon before, and that was in Hawaii where I just managed to break three hours. 2:58 was my previous best finish, so my aim was to better that in London. With the British public out there supporting everyone, I hoped I would manage to push a bit harder. Which I did. I was really pleased with 2:52.

I've also got into triathlon. It started back in 2007 when the F1 car wasn't working so well, and I thought it was nice to do something where it was all down to me as an individual. I've also made it part of my fitness training for F1 and I've continued from there. I've got an addictive personality and a competitive spirit and I've been really enjoying my triathlon journey over the years too. I've done half-Ironman distance but it's back down the sprint distance for my own triathlon which I hold every year. That's the good thing about the Jenson Button Trust Tri: anybody can do it as long as you can paddle your way around 200 metres. It's a 200m swim, 10km bike and 2.5km run – then double the distance for the finals. So for me, it's proper, full on, lungs burning for about an hour. Brilliant!

◉ Jackson Browne, *Running on Empty*

'OUTLAW' iRONMAN TRiATHLON, MiLE 10

Into mile 10, and I think I've worked out why my stomach has been hurting so much. It's hunger, pure and simple.

Well, maybe not pure and simple. Hunger, grim and tortuous might be more appropriate. And completely my fault for being so inept and unable to plan properly.

If I'm at one end of the Ironman ability spectrum with my current, paltry efforts to complete this one, Chrissie Wellington is at the other. She's raced 13, won 13. She's also four times world champion, and world record holder by masses. Chrissie once told me that if you get your nutrition wrong in an Ironman, you measure the mistake in hours. Well, I *almost* got it right.

Before leaving London and driving up to Nottingham (via 48 hours throwing up in the New Forest and a Children in Need jamboree in Sussex), I'd had the foresight to make myself a rather wonderful, super-healthy, super-nutritious superfood cake of my own devising. It's a strange-looking concoction I grant you, but I remain insistent that (1) it's really quite tasty if you ignore how unappetising it looks, and (2) it might just be the perfect endurance fuel. Just six ingredients: oats, egg, avocado, banana, blueberries and peanut butter – mash them all up and bake. It's all in there: slow release carbs (oats), good fat (avocado, peanuts, egg yolk), sugar for instant energy (banana, blueberries), anti-inflammatories (blueberries) and protein (egg and peanuts). All in there, and all good. Tastes nice too. I'm so proud of it, I submitted the recipe (such as it is) for inclusion in the charity book *Fuelled By Cake* compiled by another amateur triathlete, Helen Murray. To be honest I've had a mixed response from people who've subsequently made it – but I still continue to believe in it. Who needs a protein shake when you've got a superfood cake?

I'd wolfed down some cake at 4am in my poky hotel room as I got my race things together. It was precisely the recommended two hours before the swim start, and after forcing down as much cake as I could, I carefully wrapped the rest to eat after the bike ride.

Having completed the swim in just over an hour, and at that stage feeling quite good about life, I made the snap decision to bring the remaining cake with me on the bike.

Now what with being ill and busy and all, I'd not had a moment to buy myself any proper triathlon kit. So I was racing in the same get-up I used for my training rides up and down Box Hill: long-sleeved running shirt and baggy old cargo shorts. In a field full of Lycra, the shorts may have looked comically out of place, but they weren't half practical. Room for a puncture repair kit and hand pump in one front pocket. And, as I decided on a whim this morning, room for my cake in the other.

The mid-point of the 180km bike ride came at the top of a hill. Annie Emerson, triathlete-turned-TV-presenter, was there with a camera and wanted a quick interview. In fact she enjoyed a laugh at the ridiculous shorts more than she asked any questions, but the whole episode came as a welcome break from my by-now caustic calf. So afterwards, as I reluctantly resumed pedalling, I succumbed to the urge to treat myself to a little corner of cake.

Very nice it was too. Only one problem: I must have failed to put the rest back in the pocket securely, as that's the last I saw of my much-needed super-sustenance. At some point during the second half of the bike ride, the cake fell out of my shorts unnoticed, and at about the same time, my digestive system started to reject the sickly-sweet gels being offered by the ever-excellent volunteers manning the aid stations. I had been meaning to train myself to get used to these by using them during long ride/runs in the build-up to this, but as with so much else, somehow never got round to it. Error.

Every time I grabbed a gel and tried to wedge the glutinous liquid down my parched throat, I promptly threw it all back up again.

So the cake I was planning to scoff at the end of the bike ride became ever more important to me. As I pedalled those seemingly endless kilometres unaware of the cargo shorts pocket disaster, I started fantasising about the moment I could tuck in. It's what kept my feet going round and round in the cleats as I ticked off the distance markers. 120km, 130km, 140km... just another forty to go until cake... 150km, a little dizzy with hunger, but only around an hour left... 160km, tempted to have a little nibble just as an appetiser but no, resist the urge to enjoy it all the more when the pedalling finally ends... 170km, so close I can almost taste it... 176km, onto some cobbles, slowing the bikes down but somehow taking the pressure off, no cycling hard here, time to savour the prospect of the blissful calories to come (though the cobbles are also prime suspects in the great 'What Caused The Cake To Fall Out Of The Pocket Mystery')... 178km, it's Christmas Eve, the anticipation almost as sweet as the big day itself... 179km, back around the lake whose grandstands were deserted last time I saw them after the swim, now teeming with people cheering on loved ones, everyone smiling, everyone enjoying the sunshine (everyone but the lunatics racing, that is)... then finally, finally, thankfully, 180km, and out of the saddle, and off the bike, and no more pedalling, and a few sweet moments of rest ahead of the only triathlon discipline I was approaching with any semblance of confidence: the run.

And best of all, the cake which had occupied so much of my conscious brain for four hours. Bliss!

So it was quite a blow to be honest, when I sat down in the transition tent next to a bloke who didn't look remotely tired as he greedily stuffed down tuna sandwiches, to discover that the cake was nowhere to be seen. I checked through every pocket with an increasing sense of desperation. Chrissie's words reverberated in my mind as it dawned on me that I was going to have to run 26 miles hungry. 'Get the nutrition wrong in an Ironman, and you measure the mistake in hours.' And also, more to the point, because I'm not really testing myself against the clock today, you measure the mistake in misery.

So yes, that must be why my stomach hurts so much. Hunger. Pure and simple, grim and tortuous. All my own fault. And still 16 miles to go.

Jo Scott-Dalgleish is a nutritional therapist who specialises in endurance sports. What she is *not*, she makes clear, is an endurance sports nutritionist. There's a difference, you see. For a start they train differently, and Jo's also keen to point out that she examines her patients' overall health as well as their sports performance. Which is good, because that's exactly what I want to talk to her about. When I first started running, like pretty much all novices, I fell into the trap of believing I could eat what I liked, however much I liked, whenever I liked.

And the thing is, I have a big appetite. And I do mean BIG. If this were a children's book, I'd emphasise how big my appetite is by increasing the font size dramatically so only those three letters B I G could fit onto the page. I might also include a Quentin Blake-style illustration to hammer home the point. A picture, say, of the amount of food I can happily put away in one sitting.

Though come to think of it, I suspect you might be sitting there, reading this, supposing you have a similarly large appetite. Thinking, I can eat a lot too if it comes to it, I'm probably equally greedy. Well, take it from me (and this is a good thing as far as you're concerned), you're just not. My appetite can be obscene. I frequently eat more in a day than the rest of my family put together.

This, for instance, is what I put away from the hotel breakfast buffet every day of the 2008 Beijing Olympics. And there are witnesses – credible, dependable witnesses, BBC staff members and International Olympic Committee officials – who could testify to this.

I'd start each day with some fruit, to make me feel healthy. Two large bowls of fruit salad. Then some cereal – a large bowl of muesli, and a large bowl of something treaty like Frosties. Next, toast with butter and marmalade. All of which I considered to be a starter.

The main course consisted of a full cooked breakfast – scrambled eggs, bacon, mushrooms, beans. Then the local breakfast dish, which I always try wherever I am in the world, in this case an egg hard-boiled in soy sauce (turning the white brown and making the whole thing deliciously salty) and a bowl of chicken noodles.

To finish, I'd have some fish, mackerel or smoked salmon, on more toast, followed by a croissant to go with my third cappuccino.

I'm a little embarrassed to see that all written down. But there it is, a truly gargantuan, gluttonous breakfast, and I devoured it every morning for the 28 days I was in Beijing. Nowadays I pretend not to have a problem with how much I eat and pretend I don't worry about getting fat – but I kind of do. It's why I started running in the first place, and one of the reasons I keep going.

Nutritional therapist Jo told me:

'Many people come to see me thinking they can basically eat anything they like because they've started running. But there are several different factors to consider here, not least – what sort of running are you doing? Is it a 5k Race For Life, is it a first marathon, or are you off to do an ultra*?'

'One of the common things I see in people who are new to running is an assumption that because they have burned extra calories, actually around 300 say on a typical 20-minute jog, they can reward themselves with guilt-free treats. That's clearly an error. In fact, *that level* of physical

---

* An ultra-marathon is any race longer than a marathon, typically anything from 35 to 100 miles in a single go.

activity on its own is going to make no difference to weight loss, or fat loss.

'The type of running you're doing, the distances and the type of training, it all plays a really important part in any nutritional advice I would give. But clearly, if all you do is a weekly 5k parkrun and you reward yourself with a burger and chips, what you'll find is you inevitably end up putting on weight rather than losing it.

'Also, there is an issue over health. If you're going to be a runner and you're going to have that sort of healthy lifestyle, then what you eat for your meals and snacks is vital. It's important for immune support, because often when people start training heavily, their immune system begins not to function quite as well and they become prone to upper respiratory tract infections like colds. And there's the injury risk when people start running and become quite enthusiastic quite quickly, building up volume without increasing it slowly, and if they have a poor diet it's going to take them longer to recover because they don't have the basic nutrients they need to repair bones, muscles and ligaments. The naturally lean runners wouldn't necessarily consider that.

Are we allowed to binge on pasta and bread though? Traditionally, the runner's diet has been high in carbohydrate and you'll still hear experienced marathoners talk of carbo-loading before a race. But are they right to do so? Recent research, according to Jo, suggests not:

'A very high carbohydrate diet is not necessarily optimal for running performance, but that doesn't mean to say that it doesn't work very well for some. The Kenyans, for example, naturally have a very high-carb/ low fat diet and nobody would suggest they would do better if they ate more fat.

'There is probably a genetic component to how you personally respond to what you eat, how you react to carbohydrate and fat and how sensitive you are to those particular nutrients. But there are several other aspects of the carb-story that are coming out through research. One is that running in a fasted state, which means not having any food at all before a run except perhaps a cup of coffee, does have some benefits for endurance capability. It helps to 'switch on' the biochemical pathways that help grow the mitochondria in the muscles – essentially charging your batteries. So doing a fasted run before breakfast once or twice a week can be very helpful come race day, and it also teaches your body to run off its fat stores.

'Both the research and basic biochemistry tell us that when you're running at a certain intensity, your body has to use carbs. You simply cannot convert fat into energy fast enough to feed your anaerobic[*] energy system. However well adapted you are, there comes an intensity beyond which you simply can't run on fat. Any 5k or 10k race, as well as any half-marathon for almost everybody, and even a marathon for a fast runner, someone who'll complete the race in around three hours, none of those races is going to be run on fat stores.

'The people who are successfully teaching their bodies to run off their fat stores are doing so for the longer events where you're running at zone 2 intensity, maybe even zone 1[†], for really extended periods. For instance a slower marathon runner, and especially an ultra runner, an Ironman triathlete or an endurance cyclist doing a six-hour sportive, those are the people who can access fat stores. But when they want to

---

[*] Anaerobic exercise is the type where you get out of breath very quickly, like sprinting. Aerobic exercise still raises the heart rate, but you can continue doing it for much longer.

[†] There are four recognised training, or heart rate zones. You can estimate your maximum heart rate by subtracting your age from 220. Then, wearing a heart-rate monitor, you can know which training zone you're working in:

Zone 1: 65–75% of maximum heart rate. Low-end aerobic training. A gentle jog.

Zone 2: 75–85% of maximum heart rate. Higher-end aerobic training. You'd find it hard to have a chat whilst working in this zone.

Zone 3: 85–90% of maximum heart rate. This is the zone in which you'd probably run a 5k or 10k race, though advanced runners will spend a whole marathon here.

Zone 4: 90–95% of maximum heart rate. Anaerobic training. Flat out sprinting.

speed up, they'll find it a struggle as they don't have the carbohydrate to convert quickly into energy.'

Hearing this, I begin to make sense of why I was finding the run such a struggle in the Outlaw.

'What happened to you in the Ironman is your carbohydrate stores got completely depleted, and you hit the wall. If you were able to complete the marathon at all, the only reason is that you accessed your fat stores at that very low intensity at which you were running. If you had been able to keep your carb stores topped up during the bike by taking on, say, 60g an hour through a combination of gels, bars, drinks, whatever you had taught yourself in training to be able to tolerate, it would have been a very different story.

'The stomach is a big issue when it comes to long distance triathlons and ultra-marathons. There comes a point where you instinctively don't want to take on board any more nutrition, but you need to. That's why practising is incredibly important. You can't be on your feet, or working hard, for such a long period of time without eating.'

Now she tells me...

Chrissie Wellington MBE

Four times Ironman World Champion and world record holder. Undefeated in all 13 Ironman distance triathlons she entered. Since retiring from competition, she's helped found and promote many sporting events from the women's Tour de France to junior parkrun.

I can remember running quite a lot (informally) as a kid, and I think I drove my parents mad because I wanted to run or cycle everywhere rather than walk. I used to run around the garden with bare feet shouting, 'I'm Zola Budd! I'm Zola Budd!' She was obviously an inspiration to me at that time; it was 1984 and the Los Angeles Olympics when she competed in bare feet. She was, quite simply, a visible role model. Sharon Davies (swimming medallist for Britain) was another.

I recall doing cross country at school, not being particularly good at it but enjoying the off-road aspect of the running and being in nature. And I was quite a tomboy so getting muddy and dirty and sweaty appealed to me.

But it was all very unstructured and I didn't see running as a sport that I necessarily wanted to improve at or even become more proficient in. It was just something that I loved to do, but at the time I didn't see – or I didn't recognise – that I had any particular running talent.

Years went by: sixth form, university, and I really didn't run again until I did my Masters degree. I'd been travelling for a couple of years and had gained a little weight and had gone a little puffy! So after going round the world I arrived in Manchester and decided I wanted to run as a means of losing weight.

I had an old battered pair of trainers and I can remember being embarrassed that I went very red when I ran. I've since learned that I naturally dissipate a lot of heat through my head, but at the time I just knew I went red when I ran – so I used to go out early in the mornings so nobody would see me. I also didn't have any specific sports kit, so I'd run in a regular vest top or an ordinary jumper in the winter, along with some old cargo shorts or leggings.

But then I was inspired to take running a little bit more seriously when I was talking to my friend who'd grown up with a heart defect but had just completed the London Marathon. So I thought to myself: here I am, I have two legs, two arms and a fully functional heart. What's to stop me running a marathon?

I managed to get a charity place for London the following year – it was 2002 and places were much easier to come by in those days. So then I started running a lot more. But I still wouldn't say I knew much about it. I just went for a run.

That was the point when I first started to enjoy it, even though I still didn't know the first thing about training to improve my performance. I didn't have a clue about hill training, or interval training, lactate threshold training, fartleks.... Basically I didn't have any idea of pace. I just went out and ran for 20 minutes, 30, 40, an hour, an hour and a half... it just gradually increased.

And I ran the London Marathon in 2002 and I surprised myself by running a time that was much faster than I ever dreamt I was capable of – 3:08.

That's when I began to realise that I had a bit of a talent for running and also that it was something I really did enjoy. I had just taken part in a big event with fantastic crowd support. And it brought my family together too because they all came to the finish line and we all celebrated as a family. A fantastic day, which prompted me to take running more seriously.

So I began to focus on how to improve. I thought a running club would be the answer, but I was quite nervous about joining one because I still didn't know a lot about the sport. I thought you needed knowledge as well as talent before you could join a club. But I was really wrong about that.

In fact you don't need to know anything, you definitely don't need to be able to run a fast marathon, you don't even need the right clothes. These clubs are so open to new members, and so welcoming, and so used to empowering anybody who's new to running – and so it proved with me.

I believe I truly benefited from joining a club, especially one with such a fantastic coach. The late Frank Horwill* used to train us down at Battersea Park track – and as I started to see improvements in my running that's when I really started to love it.

I'm quite performance orientated. I like to set goals and achieve them, and watching myself improving was very encouraging. Then of course, when you discover you're actually quite good at something, it doesn't half help! I made friends in the running club, and that made me go running

---

* Frank Horwill MBE (1927–2012) was most famous for founding the British Milers' Club (BMC) with the aim of 'raising British middle distance running to world supremacy'. Before long, British runners held every single male middle-distance world record.

even more, and what began as a weight-loss activity soon also became a social activity as well as a fitness activity. I've found there are many different motives for getting involved in running and often they evolve as you develop.

Starting anything is horrible – it's the hardest part! And especially if it's a sport, and you're not fit, so it's not comfortable, it hurts and you don't know exactly what you're doing. That soon changes; you've got to be patient, you've got to see it as a journey.

That's the beauty of sport – you're always developing, always evolving, and always learning. Whoever you are, whether you're Mo Farah, Paula Radcliffe or me, we all went on that first run and you can bet your bottom dollar we all found it equally horrible. But something compels you to keep going – and if you do keep going, you reap the benefits.

◉ Iron Maiden, *Running Free*

'OUTLAW' iRONMAN TRiATHLON, MiLE 11

There's no getting away from the pain, and I'm genuinely trying everything. I attempt to let my mind wander, and look at the calm waters of the River Trent all peaceful and inviting. But then I remember I've already swum plenty today, 2.4 miles to be exact, so that's not working for me. I start again, practically forcing myself to daydream to take my mind off things.

Just then, as I pass Forest's City Ground, I spy Notts County's stadium across the water and try to remember its name. The answer would usually come automatically, as it would for every club in the English and Scottish Leagues. I'm a little sad like that. But today my mind, like my legs, is sluggish. Eventually the synapses spark and I get there, Meadow Lane. I struggle to remember if I've ever been. I rack my brains, it does look familiar...

My subsequent attempt to while away a painful minute or two sees me making a mental count of every football ground I've ever been to. Turns out 60 is the magic number. But every time I remember Wembley, the Euro96 theme tune 'It's Coming Home' pops into my head. I can't seem to get rid of it or think about anything else. *It's coming home, it's coming home, it's coming. Football's coming home...*

And then it occurs to me, this would all be so much easier if we were allowed to listen to music whilst running. You can't have failed to notice by now that each chapter begins with a running themed song, because music has been very important to me whilst running. Not always, mind you, but more often than not. And on a hard run like a marathon, it can be vital.

However, back in the transition tent, back when I was realising to my horror that my superfood cake had disappeared on me, I also discovered that this particular marathon would have to be music-free. And not because I'd forgotten to bring my iPod – miraculously, that *had* made the trip north with me. But as I clipped it onto my shorts and began plugging in my earphones, my sandwich-munching mate, through a mouthful of tuna mayo, warned me that I risked being disqualified if I was caught running with headphones. No warning, no second chances apparently, just instant disqualification. Which having come this far would represent something of a pity. Note to self: read the briefing notes in future. I was on a yellow card anyway for forgetting to put on a helmet before touching the bike in first transition, so decided not to risk it.

But I'll tell you what, with 16 relentless miles still in front of me and a faint refrain of Baddiel & Skinner & The Lightning Seeds on permanent repeat inside my head, some music to lose myself in right now would be nothing short of bliss.

A sunny Sunday afternoon, running on a towpath and looking across the river at a football ground. But this is more than a year earlier, the river is the Thames and it's the famous white Riverside Stand of Fulham's Craven Cottage dominating my eye-line. I'm not trying to remember the name of the ground, but who's playing next Saturday. And as for trying to think whether I've ever been before, no need: my son and I have had season tickets for years. We cycle this very route together every other Saturday, always convinced we're going to witness a win, and more often than not return the same way disappointed. Still, we always enjoy spending an afternoon together, as well as the enormous Craven Cottage hot dogs.

Unlike in Nottingham, this Sunday sees me enjoying a jog with the dog (not a slog), and I'm gaily listening to my music. One song ends and another begins, *'Sexy and I Know It'* by LMFAO. I had no idea that was on here, must have been added by my wife. But it's fast, it's silly, the beat fits neatly into my stride pattern and as the lyrics kick in, I even find myself starting to smile. Perfect! I'm running fast and easy, grinning a little, generally delighted with life. The chorus kicks in. Hello, I think to myself, I know this bit.

> *Girl look at that body,*
> *Girl look at that body.*
> *I've got passion in my pants*
> *And I'm not afraid to show it, show it, show it...*
> *PAUSE...*

As the song pauses for a moment, let's do the same and leave me enjoying LMFAO on the Thames towpath. I've often marvelled at how a decent tune can help you bounce along more merrily. And when I'm running to a beat and relishing the fact, like I was that Sunday by the Thames, when there's a new song on the playlist which is happy and upbeat and easy to run to, I wonder how I ever manage to cope without the iPod. It's a small red clip-on Shuffle engraved with '*The Best Dad in the World*', a Christmas present from my children. I love that iPod more than almost any other possession.

But sometimes I'll be away from home having forgotten to bring it with me, or it will be out of juice, and I'll be out running and realise how pleasant it is *not* to have music and lyrics crowding the eardrums. And in those moments, I'll believe strongly that music and running *shouldn't* mix, almost like I'm sullying the purity of the experience when I pound along to a playlist.

I once interviewed Steve Cram about this very subject. He never runs with music, and thinks it's an unwelcome distraction from the real business of concentrating on form, speed, technique, breathing... from proper running basically. And listening to Steve talk, you instinctively know that he's right. (And he's generally quite persuasive anyway.) But lower down the athletic food chain, can music actually be a good distraction?

Andy Lane, a decent runner in his own right, is Professor of Sport and Exercise Psychology at the University of Wolverhampton. He's researched this very subject and believes that music *can* help.

'Take your typical marathon runner,' says Andy. 'He or she will do a long slow run, usually on a Sunday morning. If they're doing that on their own, which most are, then quite frankly it can get a bit boring.'

I know what he means here. I tend to do my long run on a Wednesday between the breakfast show and picking up the kids from school. But I often spend the entire morning dreading the tedium. I'll arrive at work with running shorts under my jeans and the plan is always to make a quick getaway and embark on the long run just as Ken Bruce takes over the airwaves. In reality, I spend at least half an hour replying to emails that barely need reading, send out some spurious new messages of my own, get up to date with my accounting, do some light invoicing, research possible future family holidays, and use Roger Federer's US Open tennis ball (which I deftly caught at Flushing Meadows whilst watching him practise) as a trigger point massage. Eventually Alan Dedicoat, legendary newsreader, voice of the National Lottery and Strictly Come Dancing and with whom I share an office, will get tired of my tennis ball contortions and insist I leave for a run immediately.

And so to Regent's Park, which is lovely but once you know it as well as I do, a little dull; thence into Primrose Hill whose hill isn't quite high enough or steep enough to keep you interested; and that just leaves the canals, the seemingly endless, slightly smelly waterways stretching from Paddington past Kensal Green to Harlesden and beyond. Somewhere along the way I simply turn around and do the whole thing in reverse. Only I don't finish at work, I continue onwards to home – and trust me, central London to Barnes, despite Hyde Park and Holland Park and however many exhaust-avoiding side streets you go down, is dull, stodgy, dreary.

Professor Lane tells me:

'Music can help in several ways. Firstly it can be a distraction from what you're doing. So if you're going for, say, a two-hour run and it's at a slow pace (so you're not exhausting yourself and don't have to concentrate too much on what you're doing), then simply pick a two-hour piece of music you actually want to listen to, and put that on.

'Don't spend Saturday afternoon dreading the following morning's long run. Instead of feeling sorry for yourself, download a new album – or even better, go through your iPod and put together a two-hour playlist of songs you really want to listen to. Then you've got something to look forward to, you'll relish the prospect of a long run and not shudder at the thought of it.'

Good advice, but can this whole distraction thing go too far? I remember an unfortunate incident in the gym when I became so absorbed in a football match I was watching, I forgot to keep my legs turning over and almost fell off the back of the treadmill.

Prof Lane has an answer for that too:

'You simply have to teach yourself to become skilled. People often run at the gym whilst watching sport and if something exciting happens like a goal or a penalty, they'll frequently end up in an unseemly heap on the floor. But once you learn to run non-consciously, you can then safely focus on something else like the game.

'And that's actually quite a good trick to cover two hours of exercise: if you can do it without any consciousness whatsoever, your legs manage the distance and your heart gains the fitness while all your mind has done is watch a game of football. Also, if your gym has screens hanging from the ceiling, rather than as part of the running machine, then that also keeps your head up and your posture correct. Distraction, more often than not in the form of music, definitely helps.'

What about that vague feeling that music can in some way contaminate the purity of a run? A long run somewhere new and beautiful is an entirely different proposition to the canals of central London. Whenever I'm away from home, I can't wait to get out on an early morning run. I'll creep outside and lace up my trainers, desperate to discover where that footpath we drove past leads to, where this run will take me. And I largely prefer to go music-free, allowing my senses to take it all in.

The good professor agrees entirely, do run without music on holiday he says. Emboldened, I then tell him I assume speed sessions should be silent as well, and describe how I try to keep a Cram-like focus during interval sessions* and the like. But I'm surprised to learn I'm getting that wrong. Apparently mid-paced running can benefit from banging in some beats.

I'm chatting to Andy on a mobile phone's loudspeaker with noises off (on my side of the line) from my rambunctious baby daughter. I sense that this is where Prof Lane really starts to get enthused by his subject matter, and his zeal even seems to infect a seven-month-old, because Mary stops what she's doing (trying to eat the TV remote) and stares at the phone, apparently rapt.

'I'm not talking eyeballs-out running here but the reasonably hard stuff. Music can definitely help with that, and really get your cadence up. For example, if you want to go faster by having a faster turnover, you just synch your feet to a fast beat, and like a metronome get yourself in the rhythm with an even stride rate – absolutely fabulous!

'And for a classic 6 × 3 session (six three-minute sprints with three-minute jogging recoveries), you can look through your playlist and choose six fast songs, and six slow.

'For instance, *Running Free* by Iron Maiden, that's your classic upbeat, running-in-the-lyrics-type song. Perfect for a fast interval. Then pick a slow song, like *Golden Brown* by the Stranglers – bung that on for your recovery interval, and that will send the message to your brain to slow down, take it easy, relax.

'The fast song with inspirational lyrics raises arousal, which is the emotional state that helps you push through the pain. The

---

* Interval sessions involve alternating high-intensity workouts with rest periods.

trigger then comes to slow down when the brain hears something relaxing, and you're no longer trying to smash things out, you're going as easy as possible. And one of the best bits of advice for runners is not to go too fast on the recovery intervals. Do the quick ones quicker, but then *recover*. Slow songs can help you do that. They condition the mindset to switch the priority from being high-end to low-end.

'And as an added bonus, music can even time the intervals for you – a three-minute upbeat song equals three minutes of high intensity, and a three-minute ballad means three minutes of rest. Bleepers don't give the same emotional response as songs, and you don't want to be looking at a stopwatch as that's distracting.'

As my daughter finally loses interest in running reps – and I can't honestly blame her as she hasn't even learned to walk yet – and resumes her quest to eat the remote, Prof Lane concludes:

'Music conditions an emotional state that pushes the effort exactly where you want it to be. Perfect.'

Perfect?

> *I've got passion in my pants*
> *And I'm not afraid to show it, show it, show it...*
> *PAUSE...*

Let's re-join the Thames towpath opposite Fulham Football Club. In winter I'll frequently have this stretch of river to myself, but today the weather is gorgeous and there are plenty of other people about. As the song pauses, I'm about to overtake an elderly couple out for a leisurely stroll in the spring sunshine. In the spirit of the enormous wellbeing I'm currently feeling, I turn to smile at them as I draw alongside. But that's exactly when the chorus kicks in and I suddenly, unexpectedly, accidentally join in. If you know the song, you'll know that the next line is said, rather than sung.

'I'm sexy and I know it!' I blurt out, loudly and enthusiastically.

Oh no! What have I said? These poor people definitely *won't* know the song in my earphones. And the way I came out with the chorus line, more a statement than a tune, and did so just as I turned towards them – it will have seemed to them like this was something I really wanted to let them know, something I needed to get off my chest. That I wanted two elderly amblers, two perfect strangers, to know that I sincerely believed myself to be alluring.

I pause, dither, wonder whether there's any way of getting out of this. But they're now starting to look at me a little apprehensively, doubtless fearful that there might be more where that came from. I realise my hesitation is only serving to reinforce the impression that I genuinely wanted to get across the message that, perhaps because of my running and certainly to the best of my knowledge, I am sexy.

I run on, inwardly cringing. And I still wince whenever I hear that song. Damn you, music and running!

Liz Yelling

Twice represented Team GB in an Olympic marathon, and a medallist at the 2006 Commonwealth Games. Now a widely respected coach married to Martin Yelling from the next chapter.

I remember doing sprints at primary school and always feeling really frustrated that I never won. There was always this one girl who beat me. I still know her name to this day, Kristen Patterson!

But when we moved up to middle school we were introduced to cross country. I did my first cross country at the age of nine. We were running around a heath next to the school. I was a bit nervous when I stood on the start line because I'd never done it before. We all hared off and we were jostling for places and elbowing each other out of the way. But then about 300 metres further on I looked behind me and there wasn't anyone in sight; it was just me on my own. I thought, 'Oh! Where's everyone gone?!' I kept running. It must have only been around a mile and I had beaten everyone by minutes. That was when I realised that this was something I was good at.

I had a deep passion for it as well. I just loved testing myself and pushing myself. Sometimes I did have a kind of a love–hate relationship with running when it wasn't going to plan. There were always reasons it wasn't turning out the way I wanted but I always had this inner passion. Something that just kept driving me on to see how far I could take it and to see how far I could push. I could always see that there was more to come. I think that's where my motivation came from as well.

I'm competitive, both with others and also with myself. Obviously I wanted to beat my competitors but at the same time I was definitely always trying to improve and setting myself different targets.

My ideal fantasy run would be really rugged terrain off-road through forests and over mountains; somewhere to explore and see stunning scenery. Just this last week I ran over on the Purbecks near where we live in Dorset. I did a beach run I've never done before with mates, 12 miles, along some ridges with sea views, up and down rolling hills. Yeah, it's beautiful. I loved it. You just want to see what's around the corner.

For my kids, my primary objective is for them to enjoy sport or some sort of physical activity. I don't really mind what guise that comes in. I think to be fit and healthy for life is my main, my first goal. I just want to expose them to as many different sports as possible and see where it takes them. Having said that, I do look at them to see if there's a talent for running and I think Beau, one of the twin boys, he's kind of light framed and he's already fast. I've kind of earmarked him as the runner already!

⦿ Carly Simon, *Let the River Run*

'OUTLAW' IRONMAN TRIATHLON, MILE 12

I'm dimly aware that this is only the first of two riverside running laps, but I'm trying not to think about it. I'm not sure I could cope with the alarming reality that I've got to do this all over again.

To make up the mileage we cross a suspension footbridge onto the North side of the Trent, where we'll run what's been described to me as 'a short loop'. Well, it had better be short, because every step on this side of the river feels somehow malicious: it's not taking me towards or away from the finishing line; it's simply there to rack up the mileage. Simultaneously completely fair – and utterly unfair.

Surely we're going to cross the river, loop back on ourselves and head straight over again? Nope. As it turns out, we cross the river and turn left down something called Victoria Embankment. Lovely spot for the numerous couples and families enjoying a lazy afternoon in the blazing sunshine, less lovely for a would-be Outlaw Ironman who's resenting every passing metre.

At last we do turn around and retrace our steps towards the bridge. Finally! All my lingering physical problems are the least of my worries on this side of the river – my very resolve is struggling to cope. We reach the bridge, and I prepare to turn right back across towards the cricket ground.

Only we don't turn right. We carry straight on under the bridge. This loop is anything but short. And I pretty much feel beaten. The pain I could cope with, but it's getting under my skin now, this injured, undernourished marathon I'm attempting. It's eating away at my mind, my confidence.

I'm on a flight to Ljubljana, capital of Slovenia, and cousin Vassos is unusually twitchy. We're embarking on the second of our one-night European marathon odysseys, but since Barcelona we've decided we only want to run in countries we've never previously visited. (This has the added advantage, on my side, of helping me staying ahead of a pal called Tim in an ongoing game of 'who's been to the most countries'. The only rule is that you have to mean to go to that country: so a brief stop in Singapore on a flight to Australia doesn't count as Singapore, but hiring a boat in Thailand, as I once did, crossing a river to spend ten seconds standing up in Laos before heading straight back to Thailand, does count as Laos. Oh, and FIFA, football's shambolic governing body, are sole arbiters of what constitutes a country. Terrific game. You should try it. Although the friend who devised it is a BBC cricket producer, and I live in constant fear that he'll be sent to report on a long tour of the West Indies, adding, potentially, ten (ten!) countries to his tally. For now though, I'm well ahead. Thanks in part to this new marathon arrangement.)

My cousin is worried because our flight home from Ljubljana is at 4pm the following day and we've just found out the marathon doesn't begin until 10 in the morning. Working backwards, it means we need to be at the airport, half an hour's taxi ride outside of town, at 3, so we need to be in a cab with our bags at half past two at the latest. It takes half an hour to get back to the hotel from the marathon finishing line – so basically, he's worked out that if either of us fails to get round 26.2 miles in three and a half hours, we'll miss our flight home. And he's not convinced I'm up to it.

'It'll be different this time,' I tell him. 'This time I've trained properly.' Cousin Vassos remains sceptical. He has an important meeting on Monday morning, and he is genuinely worried I'll make him miss it. And more to the point, he's quick to point out that his interpretation of 'training properly' is markedly different to mine: he does two sessions a week with a professional coach, another two with his running club and a 22-mile run on his own every Saturday morning.

Fortunately, as we check into the hotel, the receptionist (bizarrely) gives us each a small toy elephant, and this mollifies my cousin. And dinner that night is epic, even by our greedy standards. We discover that Slovenian delicacies include sausages the size of your arm, hearty beef stews, tasty trout dishes, and for pudding an enormous filo pastry filled with seeds, nuts, fruit and cream cheese. We eat all of the above and wash it down with a bottle of the local red wine. Not recommended by experts, but to us the perfect pre-marathon nutrition.

The centre of Ljubljana is beautiful. Striking architecture, a green-domed, double-towered cathedral, and looking down on it all, a classic castle on top of a hill. The marathon begins right in the middle of this fabulous cityscape. An extraordinary number of people fill the narrow, cobbled streets hours before the race gets under way. The course itself is two loops through the picturesque city centre, but also meanders through quiet (on a Sunday morning anyway) industrial districts, and peaceful (all the time presumably) residential suburbs.

I feel, despite the training, like I'm running quite slowly. I'd done as much running as I could in the two months building up to this including, for the first time ever, some speed work.

There's a track near where I live, and I used it every Monday (oh, how I dreaded Mondays) to do timed 800m repeats, twice round the track as fast as possible, with a 400m slow jog to recover between each one. Ten times. The idea, devised by a famous American running coach called Bart Yasso, is to convert your 800m times in minutes and seconds (3mins 10secs, say) into hours and minutes (3hrs 10mins) to predict your marathon finishing time. All things being equal, it's spookily accurate. But the 800m (half-mile) sprints themselves are hell on earth.

Nonetheless, I had forced myself to the track every Monday lunchtime for eight consecutive weeks, and Bart's system was predicting a finishing time of between 3:00 and 3:15. Trying for once to be conservative, I start the race alongside the pacemaker with the gold-coloured 3:15 balloon tied to his wrist, and five miles in I am still ahead of him.

But I soon find myself wondering, how come so many people are streaming past me, including those who looked like they couldn't run 4:15, let alone 3:15? For the first time in my life, I wish I owned a GPS watch. My basic stopwatch, which cost £2.99 on ebay and which I could have used to estimate my finishing time whenever I passed a distance marker, is stubbornly stuck at 0:00:00. I foolishly forgot to press 'start' amid all the excitement of setting off.

By mile eight or nine, I've re-overtaken many of the slower-looking runners who'd earlier rushed by, but the real explanation as to why I'm feeling so slow doesn't become clear until half way: hardly anyone is running the full marathon. As we arrive back in the beautiful city centre, most people filter to the side and abruptly stop moving. This leaves me, for the 13.1 miles that follow, rather regretting having tried to keep up with them in the first place. And for a long time during that second circuit of the suburbs, regret it I most definitely do.

It's slightly depressing when you're aiming for a time, in my case anything under 3:15, to see the pacemaker run past you with around ten miles to go and realise there's absolutely nothing you can do to keep up. Your legs simply don't have it in them.

But the difference between Ljubljana and Barcelona was the training. This time, I'd not only started putting in some speed sessions, but I'd also done the long run mileage. So now when I dig in, there are no shocks, there's no 9km-long wall to run through. I just keep going as fast as I can, with the glorious safety net of the near-certainty that I will complete the course. The only question is how fast.

At one stage there's a 90-degree right hand turn around a large field before the road goes uphill for a few hundred metres. If you glance back over your shoulder, you can see at least half a mile of the route you've just run. I slow, almost to a stop, for a long hard look behind me and to my horror see the next pacemaker, the one with the golden 3:30 balloon, shockingly close behind and closing fast.

And that man with the balloon, it's like he represents all my weaknesses and self-doubts. The balloon of doom bringing with it, I know, real disappointment. Almost shame. For a moment, I feel powerlessness to resist, almost as if I want the balloon to pass. I'm being sucked into a vortex of hopelessly slowing legs and accelerating time.

But my response surprises me, shocks me even. I just think: *that's great, problem, opportunity... let's beat this.*

I take a moment to enjoy my unexpected, impulsive positivity and then simply go with it. *Right*, I think, *new target, stay ahead of that balloon. You know you can, so* (to borrow a slogan from a major sportswear manufacturer) *Just Do It.*

And do you know what? I did just do it. Easily.

The kilometres that had ticked by so excruciatingly in Barcelona still felt difficult, but crucially they also felt manageable. Even when I couldn't resist the lure of the dreaded 'How far have I got left to run' introspection, there was no panic. OK, I reasoned, if there are 10 miles to go, that's going to take around an hour and a quarter.... Just keep going.

And throughout those ever-demanding final half-dozen miles, I felt like I truly belonged. For the first time really, I felt like a proper runner. It was a terrific feeling. Still is.

Martin Yelling

A former England cross-country runner, he's now widely regarded as one of Britain's top coaches. Founder of the UK's number 1 running podcast, Marathon Talk, as well as the Bournemouth Marathon Festival and Yelling Performance Coaching, which he runs with wife Liz and sister Hayley, both also international runners.

I was first introduced to running in primary school. I lived in Yeovil in Somerset. We used to have an annual school cross country in a little country park in the town. I was about eight years old, and I can remember finishing high enough to qualify for the school team, which meant that I would represent my little primary school at the area championships held at the same place.

A few weeks later I went down there again, along with kids from all the primary schools in the area, and raced. I came fourth and I thought to myself, 'That's brilliant. This is something that I can do.' That was probably my first exposure to the positive inner feeling, the intrinsic feeling of success that you get as a young child where you think, 'Hey wow, I can do that.'

But moving to secondary school, I didn't take running seriously. I didn't take anything to do with secondary school seriously. I thought nothing was actually worth me bothering with. You know the mindset of a kid growing up in a less-than-stable environment. Mucking around was what I was focused on.

Running did give me something that I knew I could achieve at without really trying. When I did get some support and some help, it was my local PE teachers that said, 'Go to running club, I'll take you there.' I used to go to the running club, which just happened to be a mile up the road from where I lived in Yeovil. Some of my PE teachers would take us up there and we'd run with the Yeovil Olympiads. I qualified for a couple of English School Championships. I finished, I think, seventh in a final one year.

That was a brilliant exposure for me for the competitive aspect of running. I wasn't aware of the other benefits. But in hindsight, those other benefits were hugely important. I was spending time with my friends, sometimes just mucking around on the back of a bus going to an athletics match. They were big social occasions that I wouldn't otherwise have had. I lived with my mum when I was growing up, and she couldn't have afforded to support me and ferry me around. This was something I could do on my own, independently, and have a social life around it.

And it kept me out of trouble. Looking back, it kept me out of a lot of trouble because I would go to the running track and I'd run.

I love the space that running gives me. It may be space from other people, which isn't a bad thing. Also the feeling of space when I'm running outside, being in a natural environment, in the surroundings – even if I'm running fast and putting myself through pain and discomfort in that space.

I think about space having different forms: a personal space and natural space, an emotional space, a physical space.

That space can morph with you as you grow from a very competitive ego-driven young male athlete through to a more mature, calm, maybe a little wiser participant who loves the recreational and social side of running.

For me, it doesn't matter where that space is. I love running on the Jurassic Coast, I love running in the Lake District, I love big sky, being in the mountains, being on the top of the mountain running as the sun's coming up – amazing. At the same time I love running up a filthy set of steps at a railway bridge in the middle of a city. Or down a dingy alleyway, or along the Thames Path through little sections I didn't know were there. You look up and you can see architecture that is lost in a city. You're running through it and past it. Yeah, I just love the whole experience.

I like to run slower now and I stop. I didn't used to stop. If I see something I like, I stop because even as a runner you can sometimes be in too much of a hurry. I did a little bit of work with Eddie Izzard. He is an interesting guy to go running with. We'd stop and talk or we'd stop and look at something. And I thought, 'Well, I've come all this way in my run, I might as well stop and enjoy some of it instead of starting and stopping in the same place.'

When my wife Liz and I used to go running, we'd smash out big runs and break each other. Now we push the kids, stop for a coffee by the beach. We're still both doing something we love; it's just not quite as hard. But you've got to vary the run because at the same time I still love going out for a smack up. Putting myself on the edge. And when I finish I have to stop a few hundred metres from home and compose myself before I walk in the door so that Liz doesn't know I've been breaking myself again on a run.

⦿ Kate Bush, *Running Up That Hill*

'OUTLAW' IRONMAN TRIATHLON, MILE 13

Not even halfway through this marathon, and I'm finding the new mental struggles so much more draining than the ongoing physical ones. Ever since we crossed the river, I find myself thinking ahead, how much further there is to go, how much longer it's going to take me, how much more it's going to hurt. I squint despondently at my watch every minute or so, but the more urgently I wish away the seconds, the miles, the slower they seem to drag.

I'm told, but have no recollection of the fact, that this is when my brother Nick, kindly up from Cambridge with his family to offer moral support, decides that enough is enough and tries to call a halt to my pathetic athletic endeavours. Apparently he starts running alongside me (though by this stage he wouldn't have needed more than a brisk walk) and tells me he's seen several people pass out through heat exhaustion, and none of them looked remotely as debilitated as I do. Caroline, he adds, is seriously worried about me and if for no other reason, then I should definitely stop for her sake. I have, he concludes emphatically, nothing to prove to anyone.

Apart from being one of the kindest guys you could hope to meet, Nick is also one of the fittest. Once, on the day before the 1999 London Marathon, he agreed to take someone else's place (totally against the rules, best not to mention whose) and on zero training and having hosted a party the night before, he still managed to break four hours. The following year he entered properly, trained hard but at the last minute agreed to run alongside his wife. Once again, Nick broke four hours but this time, having wanted to go sub-three and finding himself at a loose end on the Sunday afternoon, his wife having understandably taken to bed with exhaustion, he decided to kill a few hours by going to the gym. Not for the sauna, you understand, or the steam room, or a relaxing dip in the pool. He went to the main gym for a proper workout. Having just run a full marathon. 26.2 miles in the morning; two-hour heavy weights session in the afternoon.

And if you ever go skiing with Nick, which is actually more likely than you might think as he spends every spare second on the slopes, then be prepared for the fact that he'll arrange to meet you at the top of the mountain, not by the ski lifts at the bottom. That's because he likes to wake up extra early, attach climbing skins to his skis and physically scale the entire mountain before skiing down it. Hardest of all, he's also completed paras training in the army.

So when Nick sees that his arguments are having no effect, he tells me that he's worried about me too, and in my position *even he* would stop. Now that would have resonated. Perhaps, on balance and on reflection, I might have heeded his advice.

But like I say, I have absolutely no memory of any of the above. At present I'm in my own little bubble of self-pity and all I can think about is what a long way I've still got to run. That, and whether we're ever going to cross back to the other side of this bloody river.

After Ljubljana (we made the flight home, just about), I became properly hooked on running. And whereas until then I'd merely enjoyed the uncomplicated act of going for a run, now I wanted all the gear.

Just lace up your trainers and head outside? Not me, not any more.

I was subscribing to two separate running magazines, *Runners' World* and *Men's Running*, and ravenously reading all the reviews of all the latest gadgets and gizmos.

I'm over that now, back to enjoying the sport's sublime simplicity, but looking back it feels like a rite of passage. You begin by knowing nothing, and just start running. Then you achieve something, perhaps complete a marathon, read a little, learn a little, and get a lot carried away.

So lots to do, lots to *buy*, before I laced up those shoes and headed outside.

Starting with the shoes themselves. No longer good enough to find a pair of trainers which just *felt* right, not by a long chalk. Not even good enough anymore to go to a specialist running shop, have my gait examined by a trained assistant and depending on the advice, buy a pair of comfortable neutral or anti-pronation shoes.

I accepted an offer to get my running gait assessed – in three dimensions. The traditional video camera/human eye/2D analysis is fine for detecting larger abnormalities in running style, but I learned that it's often the much smaller deviations from the 'ideal' gait that can cause injury. I found myself motoring up the M40 to a laboratory in Oxford. Friendly, knowledgeable running boffins pinned dozen of tiny sensors all over my hips, legs and feet. Then they set me off on a treadmill whilst recording proceedings with lots of tactically-positioned infrared cameras.

These measured the precise position of each of the sensors hundreds of times every second and somehow calculated my joint angles at pelvis, hips, knees and ankles in 3D. I discovered that the chief boffin, Dr Jessica Leitch, is a more than accomplished runner herself – so inwardly I beamed with satisfaction when she watched me dashing along like a hamster on her treadmill, and told me I had 'very nice mid-foot strike'. Wonderful, I thought. Been working on that. Pleased to make it official that I'm biomechanically brilliant. This trip was turning into just the sort of massage my running ego was in need of.

But what is it they say comes after pride?

The results started churning from her computer, and immediately my mood darkened. I'll spare you the details (I don't really understand them) but suffice it to say my knees were all over the place and basically, I ought to have been injured.

As I headed home through the Oxford rush-hour, I racked my brain for a solution...

Somewhere near High Wycombe a solution came to me: custom-made orthotics. Expensive, yes, but critical. I'd heard miraculous stories of people running injury-free for life in orthotics. Former England cricketer Ronnie Irani swears by orthotics to such an extent that he's now selling his own. Very good they are as well.

But I hadn't met Ronnie at the time, so soon I could be found on another treadmill in another lab, 2D this time, surrounded by more cameras and being fitted for some extremely expensive, bespoke orthotics, imported from Canada.

They also told me about a new method of sweat analysis they were working on. An athlete gets the salt content of his or her perspiration analysed, then an isotonic drink is created to exactly replicate the minerals lost during exercise. Perfect, I thought; where do I sign?

So – in between gait analysis (in however many dimensions) and perfectly balanced recovery drinks, just the run itself, right? Wrong. I had the insoles and I had the shoes, but I'd barely started.

First of all, I needed more shoes, at least another pair and preferably a different make. I'd read somewhere that it was a good idea to give the shoes (the shoes!) time to recover between runs. So the thing to do, according to the article/blog/forum I'd been reading, was to alternate trainers from one run to the next. And the change of make was to (minutely) adjust the foot strike, thereby (minutely) lessening the chance of an overuse injury. £130 to Asics and £130 to Brooks later, and I was ready to start getting dressed.

But before any outer clothing, come the base layers. As I learned through voracious reading, these are not just to keep you warm. They also, according to the blurb:

- *Deliver optimal flexibility and movement*
- *Support forearms, triceps, biceps, pectorals and deltoids*
- *Reduce muscle fatigue and damage*
- *Promote increased circulation*
- *Reduce soreness*

- *Enhance flushing of blood lactates from exercising muscles*
- *Offer core body support*
- . *Are suitable for any athletes with upper body demands*
- *UPF50+ Sun Protection*
- *Antibacterial*
- *Moisture wicking*

Oh, and they also cost £60 a pop. Not a problem, I'll take two (please don't tell Caroline). Then there are compression tights. Apparently *'injury-reducing, temperature-controlling and moisture-managing'*. Clearly completely vital. Also £90, but hey – look at all the added value I'd get from each run. Next, socks. Another £40, but that's money well spent when you consider that the ones I chose were *'not only the result of tireless research work, they were also the subject of a doctoral thesis'*. How could anyone go running without them?

Next, the shorts – *'lightweight, breathable and fast with 4-way stretch, offering the ultimate in comfort and protection'* – at £55. A running T-shirt designed to have *'a natural odour-inhibiting characteristic so you can focus on your performance'* as well as *'Next-To-Skin-Feel'* and a *'Short Sleeve Design'* – £50. Also, for winter runs *'the world's first waterproof venting jacket, designed specifically for the serious multisport athlete'* – £270. Making a total of £885, and that's just for the absolute essentials.

If you fancy, you could also own a hydration backpack *'with integrated back protector'* (£120); *'insulated waterproof'* running hat (£32); sports laces to *'improve competition'* (£8.50); compression calf tights *'for extra power'* (£35); phone-carrying, warming arm sleeves (£30); gloves *'with enhanced visibility and targeted protection against wind and rain'* (£40); head torch *'with constant lighting technology'* (£70); and a reflective *'see and be seen'* vest (£20).

And what about the watch? The £2.99 ebay number was of course no longer up to it. You see a watch doesn't just time your run. It measures current speed, average speed, distance covered, it beeps every mile, tells you how hard you're working, and even congratulates you if you achieve a personal best. So a built-in heart rate monitor is utterly critical, with GPS a given. I found one 'sleek enough to wear all day whilst qualified to guide the training of elite and amateur athletes alike'. Just the £390.

So I may have been £1,630.50 poorer (I may also be exaggerating a little; I didn't buy absolutely everything), but I was finally ready go to running.

Except I wasn't, because the watch which cost me almost £400 was still searching for a satellite signal five minutes after I turned it on. As I soon discovered, this a common problem if you live anywhere near buildings. Or trees. Or basketball players. And for a while, every run would begin with me impatiently waving a watch at the sky before setting off towards the river decked out in ludicrously expensive gear.

And far from enjoying it, every run became stressful.

A sports scientist will tell you that to improve, you need data to set goals, review progress and analyse performance. And they're right – but only, in my opinion, up to a point. I'm no elite athlete. I did by this stage have the tangible goal of running a sub-three hour marathon. But did I really need a £400 watch to help me achieve that? And a base layer, compression tights and £40 socks?

Trouble was, even during a supposedly easy run, I'd check the watch every few minutes to discover how fast I was travelling – and all too frequently the answer would disappoint. This resulted in very few of my easy runs actually being easy, because I'd pressurise myself into believing I had to achieve a certain pace. And however ropey I might be feeling, I would force myself to comply, mentally beating myself up if the miles weren't ticking by as quickly as I'd planned.

In the end, as I prepared for my run wearing every conceivable bit of kit and waiting aimlessly for my extravagant watch to find a signal, I would secretly be dreading the hour or so that lay ahead of me.

Eventually I realised that running stops being pleasurable – and stops being a release of tension, stops being an escape, an act of discovery and self-discovery – if you're constantly stressing about how fast you're travelling, what socks you're wearing and how your heart is coping.

Of course it's information elite athletes need to know. Running is their job. But for the rest of us, whether we're nipping out to burn some calories, enjoying a moment to ourselves or even preparing for a race, there has to be an element of pleasure, of diversion. And whichever way you look at it, whoever you are and whenever you're running, the fact is that you could be walking. But you're not. You're running. Running when you could be walking. It's simple and child-like and brilliant. The watch and the gear were keeping me away from that. They had to go.

As Leonardo da Vinci once said: 'Simplicity is the ultimate sophistication.'

Nell McAndrew

Model, reality TV star and author of Nell McAndrew's Guide to Running. *She has an outstanding marathon PB of 2:54.*

I've left the house in tears sometimes, literally, and come back from my run smiling and thinking, 'Right, that's how I'm going to handle this,' or, 'Here's how I'm going to deal with that.' I've left completely overwhelmed or totally frustrated, with a family situation say, or a relationship problem, and it's as if running unravels everything and puts it into perspective, gives me that thinking time so that when I get back, I've got that strength to cope with everything the best that I can. I love that. I just love it! I want to be running when I'm 80. I don't see age as a barrier.

I remember when I first started running outside. Before that, I used to do my workouts on the treadmill, setting it on an incline, but a similar, soft workout – treadmill, exercise bike and weights. I always exercised, but it wasn't until I started running outside that I really discovered that it's actually harder, because you end up running further.

There was a guy I used to train with in Huddersfield who encouraged me to run more outside and less on the treadmill. He used to say to me, 'You need to get outside and you'll really benefit more.' And I remember being dropped off miles away along the canal and then we'd simply run back. That was just to get used to running over eight miles for example, to see how your legs would feel.

The first time you do more than eight or ten miles or even a half-marathon, it takes a lot out of you and your muscles and hips feel tight. But it's amazing how your body starts to adapt the more consistently you run. And then with experience, it all begins to slot into place and you become more relaxed with your running.

Then the distance. I remember thinking about a marathon after my first half-marathon in Reading. I remember thinking, 'Oh my gosh, a marathon is twice that distance.' Now the miles don't scare me. I think initially if you tell someone who's a non-runner to go out for three miles or five miles, they'll say, 'Oh, I can't do that. I can't do that.' But once you get into it, six miles is nothing really. You can go out and run 10km without putting in too much effort.

Later I joined a running club, the Thames Valley Harriers. It was really nerve-wracking as it was an unknown. I drove there round the North Circular and I remember I was so nervous, because everyone seemed to look so fast and knew what they were doing. And I pretty much turned up in my jogging bottoms the first time; I didn't even own any running pants then. But before you know it, you get yourself all the right kit and you start to feel more part of it.

What I've also realised over the years is that every single person I've met through running has been really nice. That's the wonderful thing about it. I think it just strips down the barriers. So somebody's background, or what they do for a living, nothing like that matters. It's just really lovely, how running allows people to be themselves.

Whenever the London Marathon comes round, if I'm not running it, I'm always really excited for everybody who is. I start to wish I was doing it too, and start to feel the nerves for everybody. And chatting to different people, because you've been there and experienced these events, you can understand what they're going through. It's really exciting, but you're also apprehensive. It's just a brilliant feeling. And with me it's still always there, bubbling away inside me, and as I get older I still want to get faster. I want to pick up where I left off. To me, running is everything. It's everything.

At the moment it's just time to think, to give myself that freedom. I ran around Richmond Park recently; I haven't been there in such a long time and it felt good to be back and to be surrounded by so many other people out running and on their bikes. It gives it a real boost and there's a real atmosphere. I just love how that made me feel.

Also, it's really nice when somebody says, 'You've really encouraged me to start running,' or, 'You've really encouraged me to step up my distance and I've entered my first marathon.' When I used to go out and volunteer to be a pacer at Bushy parkrun, having somebody come up to you at the end and say, 'I smashed my PB, thanks so much' gives you the same high as achieving your own PB. It's really fantastic.

So yes, running is just good all around, for your mind and your body. I hope to be running for many years to come.

◉ Scissor Sisters, *Running Out*

'OUTLAW' iRONMAN TRiATHLON, MiLE 14

Nearly there now... almost... wait for it... wait for it... here it comes... closer... closer still... just a few more strides now, and... Yes! Done it! Half way!

13.1 miles completed. Now that wasn't so hard, was it?

Actually, who am I kidding? That was brutal. Beyond brutal. And this is only half way. Which means I've got it all to do over again. *Another* 13.1 miles. And each mile, I suspect, no I don't suspect, *I know*, each mile will mature into more and more of a nightmare as I grow more and more knackered.

And reaching the halfway point is meant to be a win.

It all began in a moment of outrageous optimism after a few glasses of wine. A little the worse for wear one evening in early December, I came home from the pub and decided to devise a training schedule for my next marathon. An actual training schedule rather than some haphazard 800m repeats on Mondays and the odd long run. It was borne of an ill-advised determination to compete with my crazy cousin, and also to test my limits a little.

So on the back of a letter from my accountant (*Hi Hugo, I do file them away too you know*) I concocted a training schedule comprising one gym session and five runs a week: a long run, two fast or interval runs and two easy runs. I never thought I'd stick to it, but basically, miraculously, I did.

Official training run number one: Monday December 12th: a trot round several bends of the River Thames to Richmond Park, followed by as many sprints up the big hill at Pembroke Lodge as I could manage (six, since you ask, though my record is 30). Then back home the quick way. Just over two hours in total.

Fantastic, I thought. What a great run. I should make a note of it, stick it in a training diary so I can see how I get on with my training week by week. And that's exactly what I did: I simply noted down that first run in a computer file imaginatively entitled My New Training Diary. Then I made a note of the 40-minute easy run the following day, and the 30-minute tempo the day after that, the intervals after a rest day and the gentle hour which rounded off my week. On Sunday evening it was positively refreshing to look back through and see a semblance of structure to my running. So I noted down the following week's efforts, and did the same the week after that – in fact, every run throughout that drunkenly devised, somewhat arbitrary 12-week plan was noted down. I'd look forward to my Sunday perusal of my weekly athletic achievements. A little pitiful perhaps, but I found there was nothing like seeing your best sweaty efforts written down in black and white to motivate you to do better the following week.

And so began a mild obsession with writing down the details of every run I've completed ever since. I honestly don't know why I bother – until I checked a few details for this book, I don't think I'd read back through them beyond looking up an old half-marathon or cross-country time to give myself something to aim at when I ran the same race another year. But somehow, a run doesn't now feel like a run until I've carefully added it to the relevant file in the Notes section of my phone. It's now called All Runs, by the way. I'm still as creative as ever with my file names.

They have evolved, these lists. At first I would carefully note down the time of day for each run, but after a few months I started to wonder why that was relevant. What lasted longer was my inclination to describe in detail which bits of my body hurt before, during and after each run, and how much they hurt. The early run list basically became a diary of my aches and pains. But as the years went by and the legs became more used to the daily pounding, I slowly stopped bothering noting the niggles. These days, it takes some serious pain somewhere worrying (knee or ankle mostly) to merit inclusion. Usually, each entry merely commemorates the length of a run (in time), its intensity (easy, hard, tempo etc.), any intervals, and occasionally how I was feeling or a mention of an unusual event.

My favourite runs to add to the list are the ones when I've explored new places. If I've really got a kick out of a particular expedition and if the mood takes me, I can almost become poetic. I've recently returned from a holiday in Dorset:

Saturday 14/2

Upwey, Dorset. On the downs, 97min hard – chilly, hilly, muddy, ruddy, lively, lovely! Had that marvellous bionic legs feeling. Valentine's Day and I just love running!

Yes, yes, I know... Reading that back, I can see how corny it is. But I relish the fact that the mere act of running can inspire such elation. And anyway, you know what? I really do love running. I sometimes wonder what my life would be like without it. Simultaneously less strenuous but more stressful, if that makes sense. And worse. Definitely worse.

Running seems to centre me, and reminds me how lucky I am. Nothing like a 40-minute blast round the river to clear your head. Conversely, if I ever go a day or two without running, I tend to become somewhat grumpy. Unbearably so, my family might tell you. I like to think I'm generally quite a cheerful soul, but whenever I'm not, it's generally because – as my kids put it – I'm either *'hangry'* (with low blood sugar level) or *'runpy'* (lack of a run-grumpy).

So as the Valentine's Day entry suggests, I do love my running. And I also love my lists. I'm a bloke, after all – and what bloke doesn't like a list. Especially a 'top five'? Top five Bond films, for instance, or top five sporting moments, cars, holidays... And now, thanks to my meticulous lists, I can look back at over a thousand carefully logged runs and start to think about my top five runs of all time.

Many were simply awesome: a sunny day in the Peak District, skipping up and down tors like some maverick mountain goat. A friendly cross-country race in the Surrey hills with a few pints at the end of it. The occasional jog round the river gossiping with a pal. And looking back, some runs were just horrific, at least on the face of it: forcing myself out of the front door onto icy pavements into a headwind so strong you barely feel like you're moving forward, fingers freezing, legs heavy, ankles aching. Yet even those have their charm. And there they all are, four-hour epics and track sessions, tempo runs and easy canters, all carefully noted down by date and timed only to the nearest minute (except when I've been trying to break some record or other).

Perhaps I should feel a little ashamed at this ongoing, compulsive list making. But I really don't. In fact I'm enormously fond of the run record. I thought I'd accidentally deleted it once, and let out an involuntary roar of despair. Some extremely quick-witted iPad–iPhone trickery from my daughter saved the day, and now the file will continue to grow as long as I continue to run. It's just there, a testament to my passion and my fixation. It makes me feel like Ozymandias:

> And on the pedestal these words appear:
> 'My name is Ozymandias, King of Kings:
> Look on my works, ye Mighty, and despair!'

Look on my runs, ye mighty, and despair!

Only you won't despair; if you look closely, you'll doubtless think, 'that's not much good', or, 'I can go quicker than that', or, at the very least, 'why on earth does he bother?' Well, I'll tell you why I bother. I run because running makes me happy, and I bother with the lists because they also make me happy. Simple as.

And like I say, all this looking back through previous runs has got me thinking. What *are* my top five runs of all time? Which, come to that, is my all time favourite?

I thought the answer would come easily but it turns out this is quite a competitive field. Trouble is, I keep changing my mind, remembering a long-ago dawn gallop on a Scottish beach, a jaunt through the stunning valleys near Rustenburg during the 2010 World Cup, a Norwegian marathon, Alpine adventure, jog through the jungle by the river Kwai... almost impossible to rank. But it does make me grateful that my trainers are the first things I pack whenever I travel anywhere.

So here's what I've come up with – the top five Rest of the World runs in this chapter, with the top five UK Runs to feature in the next. It's been tough, whittling these down. I reserve the right to change my mind in future editions...

All-time favourite Rest of the World runs, fifth place: Paris

I'd had some 'previous' running in Paris. The morning after I'd been to interview Usain Bolt, with a few hours to kill before boarding my Eurostar home, I'd happily set off for a run from the hotel, conveniently nestled at the base of the Eiffel Tower. I'd been listening to music whilst marvelling at how blissfully empty the roads were. I remembered a colleague once telling me that they shut some major Parisian roads on summer weekends, and I thought *this is the life, these French have got it sorted. Cyclists having permanent priority, and now streets closed for runners. Wow.* Through the music and my reverie, it took me some time to realise that someone on the side of the road was shouting. And not just shouting – but shouting at me. I removed an earphone reluctantly. *Qu'est-ce que c'est?* He pointed, and a glance over my shoulder told me the answer. The road wasn't closed for the good of weekend joggers; the road was closed for the Paris triathlon, and the elite cyclists were bearing down on me at full speed. I got out of the way, just about, before shamefully scuttling off down a side street to continue my run.

That's not the run that makes the top five. The run that does was altogether different. It was during a family weekend away, a happy, early morning canter along the Seine taking in many of the city's prime tourist attractions before any of them became crowded. Amazing how much of a city you can discover when you're running. In this case, the Louvre, Jardin des Tuileries, Notre Dame, Sainte-Chappelle,

Champs-Élysées, Place de la Concorde, Grand Palais, Arc de Triomphe, Eiffel Tower... Nice place, Paris. Nice run.

All-time favourite Rest of the World runs, fourth place: Triigi, Estonia.

The morning after the first night of my friend Jockey's bizarre stag weekend. I say morning; it may have been early afternoon for all I know. I woke up on the floor next to a fireplace feeling as hungover as it's humanly possible to feel. We were the only guests in a country manor house hotel where we'd enjoyed a long boozy dinner and just when we thought it was high time to turn in, we'd been shown to a summerhouse in the garden where they'd cracked open the absinthe. That's the last I remember.

The following morning's (afternoon's) run was memorable for three reasons: first, for the spectacular scenery, virgin forest interspersed with bogs and lakes – extraordinary; second, for the dramatic difference in how I felt before and after – I learned that day, fifteen years late perhaps, that you really *can* sweat out the booze; and finally, for the fact that I was chased (briefly, lazily, but still) by a wolf.

All-time favourite Rest of the World runs, bronze medal: Vancouver

The day before the opening ceremony of the 2010 Winter Olympics, and I was out by the harbour enjoying a brisk evening jog. Vancouver is a gorgeous place to go running. I spotted a man up ahead dressed in the distinctive red tracksuit of the Swiss Olympic team. He was out doing the same thing as me, running, and at around the same speed. I decided on a whim to try to overtake him, and put on a burst. When I drew alongside, he reacted by increasing his own pace to keep me behind. All of a sudden, I was in a race.

This sort of thing sometimes happens on my cycle commute to work, early in the morning, roads empty, and I admit I quite enjoy it – riding my trusty old hybrid bike with its flat tyres and clicking chain, and trying to keep ultra-light, carbon racers behind me as I pedal up Notting Hill.

But this was a whole new level. Racing an actual Olympian on the eve of the Olympics? Yes please! We were evenly matched, the Swiss jogger and I, and for a minute or two we were almost running side by side. At one point he accelerated alarmingly and I thought he had me beaten. But I somehow managed to stay in touch and the race continued. I was frequently tempted to sprint for twenty yards then turn off the seawall at the next opportunity, pretending that's where I was heading all along, and calling it a win. But it seemed wrong. This was a proper foot race, and it needed winning, or losing, fair and square. Plus, I was constantly hoping that *he'd* turn off and I could collapse and call it a draw.

We continued in this manner for at least a mile, locked in a sweaty duel, neither of us knowing who'd win, neither of us wanting to lose, and neither of us knowing even where the finishing line was.

Eventually, some eight or nine minutes into this wonderful lunacy, I sensed he might be starting to struggle. I don't know where from, but I found another gear and surged forwards, looking at him full in the face as I went by. I tried to sense from his expression whether he was beaten, but I couldn't read anything into the grimace. All I knew was, if he didn't slow down in the next ten seconds, I'd have to let him past. The whole race was up for grabs right here.

He suddenly slowed down and stopped. I was elated. A part of me wanted to turn around and shake his hand, but I feared it might come across as gloating so I continued on my way, merrily imagining I had just out-run a biathlete, a speed skater, a downhill skier…

I wish I'd never looked him up now. Turns out he was a curler. And his disappointment won't have lasted long, because when he returned to Switzerland a fortnight later, he was the proud owner of an actual Olympic medal. And all I have is an imaginary medal of the same colour to arbitrarily award a run which he will have long since forgotten.

Oh well, at least I won.

All-time favourite Rest of the World runs, silver medal: La Croix Valmer, South of France

My home run through the parks, commons and towpaths of South-West London will definitely make the top five UK list, and here's its Gallic sister. My fabulous in-laws have a small villa in the south of France, and they generously allow us to use it as our own. It's probably my favourite place on earth. The pink stone walls, the views, even the sky itself, all ooze calm and charm, and in all the time we've spent there, I don't think we've ever had a bad day.

This run can be anything from a quick half-hour round vineyards or along beaches, to several hours through some of the loveliest countryside, steepest hills and prettiest villages imaginable. And sometimes, when I'm out running there, I fantasise about moving to France and living a very different sort of life: a simpler life, smaller, maybe better, the kids attending the local school and becoming fluent in French within months, Caroline setting up an art business and becoming wildly popular and successful. And me? Well... um... Perhaps we're better off in London after all.

Gold medal winner and all-time favourite Rest of the World run: Koh Yao Noh, Thailand

The final week of a blissful month-long family holiday in South East Asia. In no sense could we afford to put our lives on hold for five weeks and go travelling, but how often do you ever get the chance? I had a month and a half to kill between jobs, so re-mortgage the house, sell the car and a couple of kidneys, grab the children and galivant off to Thailand.

We went everywhere, saw everything, even spent a night on a raft in the middle of the River Kwai and camped in the jungle near the border with Burma. That was an interesting run, the one deep in the jungle, past indigenous people staring at the running man like he was completely bonkers, and then realising why, when I returned to camp

40 minutes later and promptly collapsed through dehydration. Running in extremely high humidity, not recommended.

My favourite-ever foreign run came later in the holiday, in the final week before we returned home, when we spent six idyllic nights in a beach hut on a beautiful, unspoilt and tiny island. So tiny that one morning I decided to run around it. I woke to the sound of the waves and set off as the sun rose over the exquisite rocks jutting out dramatically from the sea (the view reminded us of Scaramanga's Island in *The Man with the Golden Gun*).

The run took around three hours in total. Following the coast clockwise, past people finishing a night's work in rubber tree plantations, past fishermen starting out to sea, past people working in rice fields, through a busy market, through gently rolling countryside, and through rain as heavy as any I've ever known, but warm, pleasant, and which stopped as suddenly as it started. And most of all, past an island school where I got chatting to the teacher who in his faltering English invited me to return with the family, which I did, and all the island children performed a song just for us while my two, then aged five and seven, reciprocated by reading them a story and reciting a poem. It was one of life's great moments.

Alistair Brownlee MBE

World and Olympic Triathlon Champion. He and his brother Jonny have been at the vanguard of the explosion in popularity of triathlon in the UK, and now run their own successful Brownlee Tri in Leeds. He's so fast over 10km that he almost entered the Commonwealth Games 10,000m as well as the triathlon.

I can't remember my first ever run, but I remember being really young, still at primary school, and being involved in a cross-country race around the school fields behind the school. Enjoying it. And then, even though I was about three years too young, wanting to take part in my first-ever serious cross-country race. It was a Leeds schools' competition for all the primary schools in the area and the rest of the kids were under 11s and under 12s. I came in about 299th. I remember it being a horrific experience, but for some reason I still wanted to do it again.

And then one summer, at about the same sort of time, I started to do quite a bit of fell running. So I'd turn up at a country show and just join in at the start – head up a hill, over a couple of dry stone walls, and back down again. I'd win £1.50, which I'd then go and spend at the sweet stall.

Then I remember the first time I wanted to train for something. I decided that I would get up in the morning and run before school. I'd have a little route that I always did: up a hill from my parents' house and back down through some woods. It was probably only about 15 minutes long. But I would get up earlier in the morning and be sure to do that before school because I simply wanted to train. That was out of choice, and I did enjoy it.

I always loved my running, and there were a few reasons for that. Firstly, I loved being competitive, and I knew that to be competitive I had to do some training so there's that. I did enjoy it. I think this is probably an idyllic, unrealistic memory of it, but being up in the early morning as the sun's coming up and birds are singing, I really did love that.

Later, when I was 11 and I went to senior school, running was a big thing there. We could go out running at lunchtime if we wanted and for me, as an 11 year old, to be able to put on your trainers and to just go out running with your mates from school at lunchtime was brilliant. I always associate running with a sense of freedom that was probably borne out of that. I think it was extremely important to me, and I've always kept that.

These days of course every training session is mapped out, but when I'm doing an easy recovery run, I just let my mind wander. And training for endurance sports is really good like that because you can just switch off and let your mind wander and take time to enjoy what you are doing. It's true that there's a purpose to a lot of my running now. But there's still the steady run, or if you're on a long run, it's still a very pleasurable, switch-off experience – simply let your legs do the work. It does get kind of difficult for me to choose new routes, to run on moors, or to go somewhere to do a run that might be really nice.... That's tricky because I'm on a tight training schedule and I can't travel so much. But I do get a bit of a chance to do that at the end of the year and in the off-season, which is always nice.

My favourite running is at home in Yorkshire, moorland running, though it actually depends on the time of year. When it's in the summer and I'm fit, I like running on smooth surfaces because you can just switch off and clock along. There's no better feeling than just running really naturally without thinking about it. It's fantastic.

But when I'm out for a really enjoyable winter run, then yeah, I love being muddy. I love being on the moors and in the elements, and then coming home afterwards and warming up.

Running is literally the simplest sport you can do. If you are starting, all you need is a pair of trainers and some clothes and you can go out the door for as little as 5 or 10 minutes and slowly, slowly build it up. Push yourself. In fact I challenge anyone not to be bitten by some kind of running bug if you can just set yourself targets and slowly improve over the first week or two. That is a fantastic thing. Almost everyone I know who has started running has at some point being bitten by that desire to do more of it and improve. It's the simplest thing I think, in any form of life: setting a goal and improving.

And it's as simple as putting on a pair of shoes and getting out the door.

◉ Sophie Ellis-Bextor, *Runaway Daydreamer*

'OUTLAW' iRONMAN TRiATHLON, MiLE 15

I've made a pact with myself to make sure I keep running between water stations. Not that what I'm currently doing looks much like running, more a curious cocktail of stagger, shuffle and hobble, but in my mind I'm steadfastly referring to it as a run. I fear bad things will happen if I start taking walking breaks. To my ever-weakening resolve if nothing else.

But each time I arrive at a water station, I do allow myself to walk (limp) whilst drinking copious amounts of water and tipping equally liberal amounts over my head. I'm not alone in doing this; it's extremely hot after all and we're shattered, but it's the reason the organisers temporarily run out of water. Nobody knew so much of the water would be doused, rather than drunk.

Whilst emergency water-buying parties are dispatched to rectify the situation, we're only being offered gels and isotonic drinks at the feed stations. My stomach has long since been rejecting these, so I'm now having to cope without any fluid. Suddenly, a large part of me simply wants it all to end. I'll wait until I see the kids, I think to myself, and then I'll make the final call as to whether or not to stop. And until then of course, the only thing to do is keep going. Keep running. I pass a waterless aid station and don't even bother to slow down.

Right then, back to Great Britain – and only GB I'm afraid, as I've yet to visit Northern Ireland – for the top five home runs (in the non-baseball sense.) I've spent an unhealthy amount of time pondering these. Trouble is, there are so many more to choose from.

My constant running companion, Holly the Labrador. She loves sticks, the bigger the better...

... and muddy puddles, the muddier the better!

My first ever race, the Great North Run, with super-chaperone Paul Smith, a.k.a. Lord of the Streak – he's run every day for, like, ever! (Paul Smith)

Finishing that first race. What a feeling! (Paul Smith)

VO_2 max test. How hard can 12 minutes on a treadmill possibly be?

…This hard.

On the start line of the inspirational Invictus Games, for wounded, injured or sick soldiers. It's a privilege to be there.

I like to think all my running rubbed off on Chris, who secretly trained for the 2015 London Marathon. He's now a confirmed runner who even runs to his Radio 2 Breakfast Show some mornings.

Favourite run of all time, the 2014 London Marathon. The atmosphere was astonishing – tidal waves of good wishes helping every runner every step of the way. (Marathonfoto)

Very lucky to have Hyde Park as part of my running commute to work. You can frequently forget you're in the middle of a massive metropolis and lose yourself among leaves like still fireworks…
(Tom Sandars)

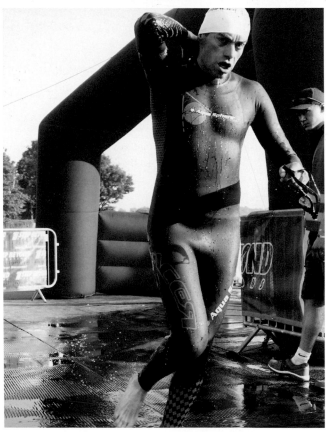

Finishing the 2.4m swim at the Outlaw triathlon. Just a 112m bike and a marathon to go… (David Pearce)

A glorious start to an unforgettable day, my first Ironman distance triathlon. (David Pearce)

Kent Roadrunner Marathon. Plan is to go sub 2:50 – so far, so good… (Kent Roadrunner Marathon (tzruns))

…but I soon I realise it's not going to be my day! (Kent Roadrunner Marathon (tzruns))

Emily (8) and Matthew (6) complete their first 5km parkrun. Proud moment.

Matthew (8) running his first 10k, representing Richmond in the Battle of the Boroughs in Greenwich Park – and loving it! Running has given both him and his sister Emily so much added confidence. (Charles Whitton Photography)

With Chrissie Wellington after a breathtakingly beautiful 13.1 miles (plus a few extra getting lost) across the Lake District. Chrissie, obviously, finished far ahead of me. (Brand Events/ Keswick Mountain Festival)

Running 100km in one go. Passers-
by look at you like you're bonkers.
They're not entirely wrong…

(SportivePhoto)

…but the feeling when you
finish is second to none.

(SportivePhoto)

At the finish of
the Windsor Half
Marathon with
producer pal Graham.
He only started
running a few months
before. I ran 19 miles
to the start and
another 19 home
again afterwards, just
to see what that was
like. (It did sting.)

Baby Mary is already showing signs of becoming the latest runner in the family!

My cousin Vassos in the thick of one of our epic pre-marathon suppers.

On Radio 2 duty at London 2012.

All-time favourite UK runs, fifth place: somewhere called Shoal Hill Common, somewhere near the M6

I'd been stuck in motorway traffic for hours, hot, bothered, barely moving forward. I was in no particular hurry but even at the best of times, I don't wear traffic jams well; it's one of the reasons I cycle everywhere in London. Eventually the car crawled towards a junction and I made a snap decision to turn off and find somewhere to stretch my legs. That somewhere turned out to be Shoal Hill Common, a large expanse of woodland and heathland on the outskirts of Cannock, north of Birmingham. And stretching my legs became a fast, undulating 90-minute thrash in some surprisingly pleasant surroundings. This run makes the list simply for the wonderful contrast between sitting stupefied in a traffic jam and sprinting gleefully up a hill.

All-time favourite UK runs, fourth place: West Sands, St Andrews

The venue for the filming of the iconic credits of the classic film *Chariots of Fire*. How much more inspirational can you get? It was early on the Sunday morning of the Open Golf Championship, I was up with the sun and had the whole curving swathe of yellow beach completely to myself. I set off for a gentle jog and couldn't help feeling that I was in the film myself... I was actually part of that happy, athletic group of white-vested 1920s Olympians splashing through the shallows: young, fit, glorying in the act of running. I was Harold Abraham, running to overcome prejudice. And I was Eric Liddell, running for the glory of God. And I was Lord Andrew Lindsay, running because I could and because I was good. I even had the Vangelis song to hand, on permanent repeat in the earphones. *Dum dum dum dum* went the insistent beat, the synthesised drum, my feet trying to keep pace with it, while the inspirational tune above it filled my ears and made my spirits soar. *Der der der dee der der, der der der dee der...*

And to top it all off, I was presently joined by some colleagues for the traditional – if absolutely freezing – BBC golf team dip in the North Sea. A breathtaking morning.

All-time favourite UK runs, bronze medal: Thames towpath, Barnes Green, Putney Heath, Wimbledon Common and Richmond Park

My home long run loop.

Depending on which precise route I choose, it's around 18 to 24 miles and to my mind the perfect combination of park, common and riverside. I know almost every puddle and pebble along the way, and love every one of them. Some days I'll enjoy the river most, racing the rowers from Barnes to Ham at the start of the run, or from Putney back to Barnes at the end, or throwing sticks into the water for my dog to flamboyantly splash in and fetch.

But if I'm not feeling the towpath, there are always the undulations of Richmond Park to keep me interested. How many times do I fancy climbing the grassy hill to Pembroke Lodge? Shall I stick to the outer path, just over seven miles of it, and try to break my PB? Shall I opt for the bridleway and enjoy the cushioning effect it has on my feet, like landing on a fluffy duvet? Shall I try to lose myself in the centre of the park? And however many times I run there and see the deer, I still get a thrill when I witness two stags rutting. You hear them before you see them, the roars and the grunts, almost human, but prehistoric-sounding, like a caveman on the charge, then you spy the antlers clashing in a colossal scrap for supremacy. Stunning. But I do tend to give them an extremely wide berth.

Wimbledon Common begins literally across the A3 from Richmond Park, and much of it is pleasantly emptier than the park and the towpath, and a little solitude can feel very welcome on a long run. But if I fancy seeing others, there's a windmill, a farm, even a golf course where the public have right of way and the players wear distinctive red tops.

Putney Heath and Barnes Green are small but close to home, ideal for adding extra little loops before heading back onto the towpath to finish.

Living in smelly old London as I do, I feel profoundly fortunate to have all of that on my doorstep.

All-time favourite UK runs, silver medal: Isle of Wight

The extended family was spending half term in a delightful cluster of cottages in the southwest corner of the island (which is the particularly pretty bit). At the time I was reaching the peak of my Ironman training and one day, as my wife, kids and a dozen or so in-laws all trooped off happily to the pub for lunch, I grudgingly headed in the opposite direction, towards the downs, to embark on a scheduled long run. I didn't much feel like it, and it didn't start well. My legs were still suffering the effects of a long Brick session (bike ride followed immediately by run) the previous afternoon. But after cutting across some beautiful coastal moorland and continuing upwards, towards the top of another hill, my legs – suddenly and inexplicably – began to feel as light as air. Running became genuinely effortless. It was the first of what I like to call my (all too infrequent, sadly) 'bionic legs' moments. I was fast, I was strong and I was free as I flew upwards past a man in tweeds out walking his dog near the Tennyson Monument. 'Ah yes, well done young man!' he called after me, 'I used to be like you once, skipping up and down here for fun.'

Nobody had ever complimented me while I was running before. I thanked him with a huge grin splitting my face. With my 40th birthday on the horizon, I was especially grateful for the 'young man' comment. But the whole exchange just seemed an emphatic endorsement of my decision to get fit and become a runner. There was a renewed spring in my step as I crested the top of the down and continued on.

There were pristine cliffs on one side of me, rolling hills falling away sharply towards the sea on the other, while up ahead the island itself seemed to reach some kind of epiphany as it narrowed and pointed towards its famous Needles, the huge white bits of rock rearing majestically out of the water one after another. Not much will have changed here for hundreds of years, I remember thinking. Back in the day, it wouldn't just have been a younger version of my friend the dog walker who was out running here, but also his parents, grandparents, generations stretching back centuries.... Running seemed to be simultaneously connecting me to my surroundings, and to the past – to those people who'd been out doing exactly what I was doing, running over the same grassy hills, enjoying the same scenery, almost tripping, for all I knew, over the exact same rocks, many years earlier.

That, and the fact that my legs continued to feel invincible for the whole four hours, puts this run very firmly on the podium. In fact it would have won gold if it weren't for...

Gold medal winner and all-time favourite UK run: London Marathon

Having been offered and gratefully accepted a media place the previous October, I proceeded to completely forget all about it. This might seem like a ludicrous thing to do (and it is) but mitigating circumstances are as follows. I'd tried and failed to get in through the ballot, and accepting a media place involved nothing more taxing than replying *yes please* to an email and filling in a brief form with my name, date of birth and next of kin. I was also looking forward to several cross-country races during the winter, and on the morning in question, casually decided I wouldn't start training properly for London until late January/early February. Well, as my wife will tell you (whilst sighing, no doubt, and rolling her eyes) I can't remember what I'm meant to be doing from one morning to the next, let alone from one season to another.

So it came as a bit of a shock when the organisers got back in touch a fortnight before the race to ask whether I'd like to interview Mo Farah, who'd be making his debut over the distance. And by the way, they asked, *how's training going?*

Training! I'd done absolutely nothing!

Well, absolutely nothing, relatively speaking. I'd still been out running almost every day. But the speed work I'd envisioned the previous October in a bid to finally break three hours on the streets of my home town? That simply hadn't happened. Neither had the increased mileage you'd usually associate with the month or two leading up to a marathon.

I'd been busy with radio in the morning and TV in the evening and the longest run I'd managed since the start of the year had been just over an hour and a half.

That same day, I ran home from central London via most of the capital's northern and western suburbs. Three hours 19 minutes, and that was pretty much all the bespoke training I managed. After that, I felt I ought to start to taper (though as my family enjoyed pointing out several times during marathon week, I'd been successfully tapering for months).

I was never tempted to pull out though, and didn't seriously doubt I could complete the course. But I *was* a little concerned that I'd end up being slightly embarrassed by my finishing time. A media place in the London Marathon is quite a public arena when you've not properly prepared.

Sunday morning dawned almost perfect for marathon running, and the sunshine persuaded even more spectators than usual out onto the streets. In fact they were lining the course four or five deep most of the way round the 26.2 miles. Over a million people in total, all of them awesome.

I can't express it better than Michael Owen, former England striker and World Cup hero, who, like Mo, was running his first-ever marathon. As a professional footballer turned racehorse trainer and pundit, you may be surprised to learn that he receives an awful lot of abuse. Much love too, but lots and lots of abuse, mainly on social media, and frequently in person. From angry fans of any of his previous clubs' rivals, from angry fans of any team he mildly criticises on TV or radio, from jealous people, from ignorant people... It can be difficult to continually shrug it off. But the London Marathon, he told me, restored his faith in human nature. What a lovely way to put it.

And he's right. If you want to see humanity at its best, just head for the Mall on London Marathon Sunday morning. Because both on the road and all about, it's only good. The runners themselves are full of determination, grit, fitness, a cheerful refusal to give up in the face of adversity, and a sincere dedication to a quest which more often than not is charitable as well as personal.

And around them are tidal waves of warm wishes. People don't tend to set out to watch a big city marathon filled with cynicism. Or to any marathon, come to that, or indeed any running race, from a junior parkrun upwards. People go to clap and cheer and support, and nowhere do they do it more loudly and in greater numbers than in London. When you're running, it's deeply humbling.

That's why I have such fond memories of the London Marathon. I'd been apprehensive at the start, but as it turned out my lack of training was a blessing. It meant I could jog round without any time pressure and simply soak up the atmosphere. It meant I could meet people and have quick chats on the way round: where are you from, why are you running, what time are you hoping for? And when I crossed the line in 3:13, around ten minutes slower than I'd been hoping for but easily fast enough not to feel embarrassed, I vowed I'd return the following year – not as a runner, but as a spectator. I wanted to make sure I was the one offering cheers, love and Jelly Babies when the runners needed it most. It seemed only fair.

So that's exactly what I did 12 months later. Despite a late, boozy party the night before, I was up at 6:30am to complete a long training run – my next marathon was five weeks away – and by 10:30 I had the family on the tube heading towards the Embankment. We bought a dozen bumper packs of Jelly Babies, joined the crowds lining the route and spent the next two hours applauding, encouraging, cheering, and handing out sweets. And eating quite a few ourselves. But the experience of clapping and giving proved even better than the previous year when I was running and receiving.

The London Marathon is simply us at our best. That's why it's number one.

Jonny Brownlee

World Triathlon Champion, World Sprint Triathlon Champion, Olympic medalist. When fully fit, he and brother Alistair, Olympic and World Champion, have simply dominated the sport. A strong believer in running on different surfaces to develop strength and balance.

I can't remember going out for my first ever run. My main early memory of running was when I entered the cross-country race for the whole of our primary school. I was only in Year Two, so I'd have been 6 or 7. The race was on a Thursday lunchtime and I just turned up for it. I felt like I was just running around, but I ended up coming second behind Alistair. That was a massive shock to me. That was my first proper race.

In fact before that I used to swim so I hadn't actually run all that much, just kind of running for fun. And I remember that school cross-country because in my mind it was enjoyable more than anything. Going out and running around the school grounds, around the playing field, up and down the hills, and that feeling of achievement when you finish.

That still stays with me now, absolutely. It's changed a little bit, it's got a bit more serious, but that sense of achievement at the end of a run does stick with me. And it's such a simple sport. That's what I've always enjoyed about running. The fact that all you need is a t-shirt, some shoes and off you go. You can do it anywhere you like. And you can always fit a short run in, whether you want to run for 20 minutes or 60 minutes or 90 minutes. You can always fit it in.

I do actually miss running for fun a little. Nowadays, my running is always training. Since I've started training properly, every single run I do has got to be for a reason, the recovery run, or a track session. I rarely get the opportunity to just go out and run for pleasure, which is a shame really.

But the really slow runs, the recovery runs, you know, the ones that take about an hour – I still enjoy those, definitely. I like to explore new areas and just go where I want. And when I'm running, then I might be thinking about anything, really. The world, just normal things, absolutely anything. I don't really think about technique or anything like that. Just random thoughts.

And sometimes running can help to clear my head. I can start a run thinking about something, and I can end up thinking about something completely different. That's the great freedom of running, how it can clear your head, definitely.

My perfect run would be to start in a small forest and up a small hill to get me going (you always want to start up a hill to get the muscles going). And then I'd run on to the top of a beautiful moor so I've got great views of the valley. And it's a nice soft surface, a grassy surface. There's lots of beautiful views and river crossing or two, and a lot of change in the scenery – a bit of moorland and a bit of forest, but all very soft underfoot. No music for me, I'm just taking in the birds and the environment and just thinking my own thoughts. No music, and no Tarmac, all completely off road. And then it finishes down a little hill. That's my perfect run. And your dinner always tastes a thousand times better after a run like that.

🌐 OneRepublic, *Love Runs Out*

'OUTLAW' iRONMAN TRiATHLON, MiLE 16

I wish I'd thought to bring a cap. In my mind, I don't need one. In my mind, I am a swarthy Greek who doesn't burn and who certainly doesn't need to wear protection from the sun in the northern English Midlands. But I'm wrong on all counts. Almost all counts; I'm right about being Greek. But swarthy, not so much. I was born in London and despite spending almost every day of every childhood summer in Greece, the British winters won and robbed me of any claims to swarthy. I even burn on holiday faster than my blue-eyed, fair-skinned English wife. So yes, I wish I'd thought to bring a cap. Absolutely everybody else is wearing one. And it's not just the burning issue I'm fretting about on this baking hot day, the athletic exertions are proving much more tiring in the full glare of the sun.

I've been thinking about the cap situation on and off for 15 miles, ever since removing the bike helmet and starting the run, but now, remarkably, as I round a corner, I notice a discarded cricket-style hat, dirty-white and a little saggy-looking, just ahead of me in the scrub. For a brief moment, I consider that it may be a mirage; it's just too perfect sitting there invitingly on a bed of nettles and offering me the chance to spend the next 10 miles under its shade. But it isn't a mirage, and its presence feels like a minor miracle.

Only slight issue: if I took it, would it technically constitute stealing? Possibly. It doesn't look like someone will come back for it, but then again if one of my kids found, say, a football in similar circumstances and asked me if they could have it, I'd most certainly tell them no. I'm therefore on fairly shaky moral ground if I want to take the hat. I can't pretend, even to myself, that I would merely be borrowing it, if for no other reason than after a few minutes on my blood-, sweat- and dirt-encrusted head, nobody in their right mind would want it back. Annoyingly, agonisingly, I conclude that the right thing to do is to leave the hat where it sits and continue without it. After all, I've got this far without one. Better to carry on with my head held high, even if that head is exposed to energy-sapping heat and relentless sunshine for another 10 miles.

Yep, decision made then: don't take the hat. It's emphatically the wrong thing to do. Better to be true to yourself, follow your conscience, and leave the hat where it is.

Obviously, I take the hat.

One of my favourite things in the world is parkrun. For the uninitiated, a parkrun (one word, small p) is a free, timed 5k run held in a park near you every Saturday morning at 9am. In our family, we're regulars.

Imagine the London Marathon, scaled down to around 10% of the length and 1% of the general size – but every bit as good. This isn't a big national event held annually and televised live on BBC1; this is lots and lots of equally laudable small events held simultaneously all over the country, whatever the weather, every single weekend of the year. Every run is completely free to take part in, and staffed entirely by unpaid volunteers. Again, running brings out the good stuff.

Which is why Saturday morning round ours looks something like this. We all wake up whenever the first child does – usually the baby, and usually annoyingly early. All pile downstairs for a small breakfast, mess around for a while, maybe get started on some homework, and change into running kit by around 8:30. Then we grab the dog (because dogs, brilliantly, are welcome too) and head for one of the six parkruns within about a parkrun's distance of our front door.

By we, I mean the two older kids, 11-year-old Emily and nine-year-old Matthew, and me. Occasionally Caroline joins us too with baby Mary in the buggy, which then gives me the chance to leave the kids with their mum and try for a rare 5k PB.

But nine Saturdays out of ten it's just the three of us, and our tacit agreement is that I'll always run with whichever child is slower on the day. They're about the same speed, my two, so on any given morning that could be either of them. It's surprisingly difficult to predict which.

We'll all set off together and before long one of the kids will kick on and the other will start falling behind, so one disappears off ahead whilst I have a pleasant jog and chat with the other. It's all smiles at the finish, then straight to the local baker for croissants and home for a big family breakfast. And by 10:30 on Saturday morning, while many families may still be dithering and lingering, we've taken the dog out, exercised together, eaten together (even the baby gets a croissant), and we're ready for whatever the rest of the weekend has to throw at us feeling like we've already won. And if anyone gets a PB, we upgrade those croissants to doughnuts.

But parkrun doesn't stop at getting people active. It's also about the atmosphere, the all-encompassing positivity. Very different to a junior football or rugby match, where there are increasingly large problems with pushy parents screaming on the touchlines, criticising referees, berating coaches and hollering at their offspring and others to *Tackle! Shoot! Come ON!* Even at the Friday evening five-a-side league my son plays in, I'm appalled by how much victory seems to matter to the parents. Not to the kids, mind you, but to the parents.

But then the following morning, during our Saturday parkrun, the change in mood is all the more striking. There you'll see mums and dads cheerfully encouraging other people's children – even those overtaking their own. Because a run isn't, and certainly shouldn't be, all about winning. It's about being the best *you can be*. And at parkrun, people seem to get that.

And then you've got the volunteers, parkrunners all of them, sometimes injured but usually not. They're there lending a hand because they know the system relies on people giving up the odd Saturday morning to help set up, marshal, keep time, applaud, run to a certain pace, bring up the rear or post the results online. Volunteering once every ten runs is the unofficial rule of thumb, but you'd be surprised by how many people do much more. It's fabulous.

Tom Williams is managing director of parkrun, and has overseen its extraordinary explosion in popularity since he first got involved in 2007. I've never met him in person, but he's remarkably engaging when you speak to him via Skype and within a few minutes it feels like I've known him for years. I ask him how he first got involved.

'Long story, but I was working in a gym and got a job at Leeds University as a lecturer in sport and exercise science. I became aware of parkrun through an advert in *Runners' World*, and at that stage there were only three of them, all in London. There was Bushy parkrun, the original one founded by Paul Sinton-Hewitt in 2004 and called Bushy Park Time Trial at the time, as well as Wimbledon and Banstead. And when I saw that ad, I thought what an amazing idea. I'd love to do something like that in Leeds, not for my own running, but just because I thought it would be a wonderful community project.'

However, the big question for Tom was *how*. He struggled to get his head round the concept of people volunteering every week. At that stage, it was simply impossible to imagine. When he mentioned setting up a Leeds parkrun to his wife, she thought he was joking. *Volunteers every week?* She exclaimed. *Not a chance!*

But then everything seemed to fall into place when he was invited to a big university meeting.

'I was representing the sports science department, and heard how the physical activity department, the non-academic side, wanted to engage the students with the community around volunteering and sport. I just thought – bingo!

'So I simply wrote the delivery of Leeds (now Woodhouse Moor) parkrun into the sports science degree at Leeds University. And at the stroke of my pen, we instantly had 140 volunteers! The idea was to engage the university students, who mostly came from affluent backgrounds, with a much less privileged local community. And it would also allow them to gain practical experience of the life-changing benefits of physical activity, in this case through running. They could learn as much as they liked in a lab, but until they saw someone lose five stone before their eyes, and gain confidence, make new friends and get fitter, they'd never genuinely understand it. That was seven and a half years ago and it's still going strong.'

Except that 'going strong' is a colossal understatement in this instance. By mid-2015 more than seven million individual parkruns had been completed by three quarters of a million different runners at 50 thousand separate events across 600 locations in over a dozen countries. At many venues there are also junior parkruns, 2km on a Sunday morning for kids aged 4–14. There are Christmas Day parkruns, New Year's Day parkruns, Easter parkruns, fancy dress parkruns, anniversary parkruns. Complete 10, 50, 100 or 250 of them, and they make a real fuss of you and give you a special T-shirt with the relevant number on the back. For free. Sometimes, you also get a cake.

Tom Williams

Managing Director of parkrun UK, and co-presenter (with Martin Yelling) of the excellent running podcast Marathon Talk. A very decent runner in his own right, having once (just about) run a mile in under five minutes.

I hated running at school. There seemed to be very little concept that you could get better at something. You were just as good as you were. So because I came last, or nearly last, in the one-mile run we once did in the freezing cold in our pants, I was always seen as not being very good at running and that was it.

Fast forward a number of years, and I was a 25-year-old student at university. A complete non-runner, I was much more sociable than sporty. But then our next-door neighbour's four-year-old daughter was diagnosed with leukaemia. I'd always had this vague bucket-list thing of doing the London Marathon. Not as a serious runner, as a charity runner – sign up, get round, tick the box, never do it again. And basically, that's what

I did. I gave up drinking for three months, I signed up to raise money for leukaemia and lymphoma research, ran it in 3:53 and never thought I'd run again.

In fact three years went by before I ran another step. I'd been round the world as a backpacker and had got really out of shape. My now wife Helen was a friend at the time and an experienced marathon runner. She told me I was overweight and unfit and took me for a run in Leeds from the local gym.

I think we covered about a mile in 11 or 12 minutes – and that was it, I was done! I was in pieces, and had to walk back to the gym with my tail between my legs. Fair to say it took me a while to get my running legs.

For my Marathon Talk podcast, I recently spent several months training specifically to see how quickly I could run a mile, and came in at five minutes dead (though the guy timing it is a notoriously slow button-presser). So I've become a decent enough runner, but these days I get infinitely more satisfaction seeing the person who never would have exercised take part in a parkrun and struggle round in 40 minutes, compared with the guy who can turn up on a Saturday morning and smash out a sub-14 minute 5k.

In fact there's a young man called Amir from the local community in Leeds. He was 12 years old when he showed up in the early days having seen us out of his bedroom window. I don't know if he'd ever done any exercise before. But six years later I was immensely proud to present him with his 250 T-shirt. So if you think about it, 250 Saturday mornings doing 5k runs, it means his entire youth, all of his teenage years, were punctuated by parkrun.

◉ Tom Petty, *Runnin' Down a Dream*

'OUTLAW' iRONMAN TRiATHLON, MiLE 17

Utter bliss! It's nice but naughty of course, and even now, somewhere in the back of my mind, I know it's wrong. But I don't care. Having a hat feels fantastic!

Technically I may even be guilty of theft, but again I don't care. It's amazing how a simple item of headwear can alter my mood and lift the general gloom. For the first time all day, after hours of steady deterioration, my situation has improved a little. It's a small thing, but noticeable. The shade from the hat is making me a tiny bit more comfortable than I was before. That's all: a tiny bit more comfortable. But it's enough to give me a significant mental boost.

And although I feel better, I know I must look even odder: the only competitor *not* wearing bespoke triathlon gear (apart from the bloke in an all-in-one bodysuit, but that's his *thing* – I'm just inept) is now topping off his ill-fitting running outfit with a tatty old cricket hat. But as I say, I simply don't care – neither about how I look, nor about having conceivably committed a minor crime.

The miles-to-go column has ticked down into single figures, I'm close to reaching the lake where I'll see my family again and where I've decided I'll make a definitive call about whether to stop or carry on, and under this hat, my physiological system is minutely less stressed than it was a moment ago. Put simply, I'm a bit less hot.

It's like being two sets down at Wimbledon, and a break behind in the third, when suddenly, from nowhere, you break back. Still a bad situation, still critical, but not quite as terrible as it had been.

Oh, and speaking of tennis, I wonder how Andy Murray's getting on...

How hard, I wonder, can 12 minutes on a treadmill possibly be?

I've come to a gym in West London for what I initially thought was to be a quick chat with the renowned running coach Rory Coleman, but turns out to be a training session. I've been put in touch with him ahead of an off-road ultra-marathon I've entered, and first up, he tells me he wants to test my fitness. This prospect initially sounds horrendous, but I'm relieved to learn that it involves nothing more strenuous than running on a treadmill, with no incline, for 12 minutes. *Nothing to worry about*, he reassures, *just 12 minutes*.

I'll take care of all the controls, so all you have to do is run.

Five minutes in, and I'm still able to continue chatting. I do have mild alarm bells ringing in the back of my mind, something to do with Rory's expectant demeanour, but there are only seven minutes remaining for goodness' sake. Seven minutes. I can take anything for seven minutes.

A minute later, halfway through this fitness test, I'm no longer able to talk easily – but I'm still content enough as I gallop along. This feels a little like the time I went to the GP complaining of heart pain, and was sent to Charing Cross Hospital for an ECG, an exercise tolerance test to determine or rule out the presence of coronary problems. On that occasion, wired up to several monitors, I had barely broken sweat on the treadmill when the staff decided enough was enough and turned it off – just when it was starting to get interesting. It turns out I was having stomach acid reflux, not a heart attack, and the ECG people had non-hypochondriacs in their waiting room. But here in Acton there are six minutes to go and I'm feeling fine. Bring it on Rory.

Rory brings it on. He turns up the speed dramatically, and watches with interest as I disintegrate.

Minute 7: Horrible, I'm running too fast, there's no way I can sustain this speed. But I can no longer speak to convey this information, and I'm beginning to realise what those alarm bells were all about.

Minute 8: *Please... slower... please...* I gasp, taking large lungfuls of air between each word. Rory tells me that grimacing and looking down aren't helping, and that I should relax and look up. And I think

Oh shut up! He also promises to help me out when I reach 10 minutes. Those are his exact words: *I'll help you out at 10 minutes.* It's not much, but I greedily hang on to that promise.

Minute 9: I'm now properly struggling, my face is contorted into a mask of pain and it takes every last ounce of effort to watch those seconds tick by slowly, excruciatingly, until at last they reach 9:57... 9:58... 9:59... 10:00. Finally! He's finally going to help me out...

Minute 10: Rory makes the treadmill go faster. Faster! *There you go*, he says. It's a mark of how much I'm struggling that what comes out of my mouth, inasmuch as I'm able to speak coherently at all, is a volley of expletives and abuse. I rarely swear. And I never swear in front of someone I don't know well. As for insulting someone who's a bit of a legend – well that's completely off the radar. But as he turns up the speed towards 20kph, I give Rory the full double barrels. There's not a chance I'm going to make it through this minute, and then the next, and another after that, at this insane pace. I'm about to hit the Stop button myself when Rory senses the rebellion and slows the treadmill infinitesimally. I somehow continue. I'm hating this.

Minute 11: A furious battle is going on inside my head. On the one hand, my self-preservation instinct is demanding that I put a stop to this absurdity. I know that I'm not able to sustain this level of effort for more than a few more seconds. I urgently want to press the kindly-looking red button in front of me. But on the other hand, it's embarrassing to give up and I'd be ashamed of myself if I did. Oh what to do, what to do? Please let this end...

Minute 12: Probably safe to call this one of the longest minutes of my life – and the longest outside of a hospital housing one of my children. I can't honestly tell you much about it. I vaguely remember it starting, and mentally taking a small amount of consolation from the fact I had less than 60 seconds remaining. And I think Rory probably did some speed control-juggling to keep me going. And I definitely remember giving up the ghost half a second early and lunging for the mercy of the red button. And then, almost as bad, the long moments hanging off the machine, gulping, gasping, heaving, wheezing, desperately trying to recover. I had been broken, utterly broken. In 12 minutes.

I'm soon to discover that what I've just been put through is called a VO_2 max test. It measures fitness through pushing your body to its absolute limit and measuring oxygen consumption. Elite athletes are occasionally subjected to these tests, but not often. Having said that, Olympic rowing champion James Cracknell has, I'm told, done over fifty. I honestly don't understand how. The first time you don't know what's coming and simply react. But after that, how do you persuade your brain to allow you to return to the well and dig as deep again when every instinct is telling you not to? That, I suppose, is what separates the athletes from the amateurs, the men from the boys, the Cracknells from the Alexanders.

Rory does some calculations to bring up the results, which for a 40-year-old ex-smoker are surprisingly good: 64.05, elite cyclist level. Delighted with that. The drawback comes as he extrapolates from the numbers – it seems I've been universally underperforming. Apparently I should be able to run 5k in 15:38, 10k in 32:37 and a marathon in two and a half hours. Not a chance in hell, of course, but interesting to know.

And anyway, no time to dwell on these revelations, as the fitness test continues. Rory goes on to suggest upper body and core-strengthening exercises before introducing me to what he calls his 'Treadmill Power Hour'. It seems to be a cross between a tempo run and an interval session, and designed to increase speed stamina. Like the name suggests, it's an hour on the treadmill – but split into twelve chunks of five minutes. Each segment consists of four minutes' running a little too fast for comfort (in my case 15kph with a 2% incline), followed by a really quick minute (17.5kph). Repeat times 12. That means you recover from each of the dozen near-sprints at around marathon race pace – and that means it hurts.

When I first started doing it, I was surprised at how deep I had to dig simply to complete the hour. Occasionally I had to stop and slam the big red button after 50 minutes. And afterwards, it would take my calves three days to stop aching. Once, I completed a Power Hour at the end of a punchy six days involving three very long runs and two attempts to break my work–home record, and managed to overtrain myself sick.

But then again, that cold came after my first 100-mile training week and did feel a little like a snotty rite of passage. First time you suffer from a repetitive strain injury when you start running? Especially if that injury is Runner's Knee? Same sort of thing – it hurts, but strangely makes you feel like you belong. Like you've joined the gang, and a very happy, sweaty gang at that. This cold made me feel like I'd joined some kind of elite running gang, even happier, even sweatier... and currently a bit bunged up.

What it also did was reinforce an idea that had been reborn the moment Rory read out those numbers after my VO_2 max test. A marathon in two and a half hours, you say? Well, even if that was so optimistic as to be verging on the delusional, it did remind me that my quest to run sub-three had fallen two minutes and 12 seconds short of being able to be described as successful, but might just be worth revisiting. I'd abandoned the whole enterprise a couple of years earlier when I found myself failing to enjoy my races, especially the longer ones. The marathons themselves had become miserable. Everything was so orientated towards that one goal that I'd lost sight of why I was running in the first place – similar to when I became too wrapped up in all the high-tech gizmos, but with a sharper edge.

It all reached an unhappy climax when I found myself slightly behind target time as I passed half way in a marathon, and essentially gave up and sulked my way to the finish. I also realised that there was no real difference between someone who could run 3:02:11 and someone who managed 2:59:59. Unless you're looking to *win* marathons, a couple of minutes barely matters. Toilet breaks last longer. And going the other way, 3:04:23 and 3:02:11 feel practically identical.

But it was my holy grail, a marathon finishing time starting with a two, and it took me a while before I realised it was making my hobby a touch joyless. So I ditched the stopwatch, began trail running, and never once regretted my decision to give up trying to shave 132 seconds off my road marathon time.

Until now. Perhaps that marathon monster was stirring once more.

Helen Skelton-Myler

TV presenter on everything from Blue Peter to Countryfile to the London Marathon Highlights Show (whilst simultaneously running the race). She's also completed several incredible challenges for Sport Relief, including a gruelling Namibian ultra-marathon.

The first event I ever did was the Great North Run in 2005. My cousins and I had seen it on TV, we thought it looked like fun, and we just thought we should have a go. I was just really impressed at the atmosphere; it always looked really good on telly. So I said, 'I'm just going to give this a whirl and see how it goes.'

The longest I ran in training was about seven miles. And my Great North Run itself wasn't quick. I think it was 2:37, or 2:39, but I just loved it. The atmosphere and the environment, and it's very humbling isn't it, because you're running along next to people who are running for their parents and children. The best bit is when you get to South Shields and there are old ladies with bags of boiled sweets calling, 'Come on, pet, you can do it.' And it really does make a difference, because when people look you in the eye and say, 'Come on, you can do it,' then you think, 'Yeah, okay, I don't want to let you down. Yeah, I'll have a go.'

The next day I could hardly walk, but I was so proud of the fact that I was limping, because everyone was asking why, and I could say, 'Well, actually, I did the Great North Run yesterday.' It gave me a real appreciation of the fact that absolutely anybody can take these things on. People sometimes say to me, 'Oh, I can't do that! I'm not the right shape, or age.' I remember looking around at the start line and thinking, 'He's massive, and she's old...' Honestly, when you go to one of those events, there is no typical body. Unless you're at the front, with the elite runners, obviously!

But I never did much running again until I signed up to do an ultra-marathon when I was on *Blue Peter* in 2008. 78 miles in 24 hours. At the time I wasn't really running at all. I had never done a marathon, but I think that was good, because I didn't realise how hard it would be to do three.

After I signed the agreement to do it, I ran ten minutes from my parents' place, and I was nearly sick. My mum and dad said, 'Is this a good idea? Do you really want to do this?'

And I replied, 'Well, I've said I'm going to do it now. I'm not going to go back into work and back out, so I have to do it.'

When I went to training events, everybody was telling me that it takes years to train for an ultra-marathon. 'Oh, you're a girl, and you're five foot three. You'll never finish that.' Just really patronising. But to be honest, the doubters are what got me through. Also, the logistics people had bets on when I would drop out, and didn't even include the possibility that I might finish. When I found that out, that was a really good motivation for me. That was the best thing they could have done.

People think that in Tellyland, it's all a bit fake and you don't really do it, don't they? They think you get a lift or something. Well we do really do it, and when I got to the finish I was totally done. I was so dehydrated I was hallucinating.

Nowadays when I run, I love the feeling afterwards. For me, going for a run, as you close in on the home stretch, that's just like the first drink on a hot sunny day – it's the best feeling ever. That's why I run.

In fact nowadays I run a lot more, especially when I'm away with work, because I like to see where we are. I like to see what's around the hotel, to get an idea of the lie of the land. And also, I think generally I like running because it lets me enjoy my food more.

◉ Flo Rida, *Run*

'OUTLAW' iRONMAN TRiATHLON, MiLE 18

I'm about to see my family again, decision time is approaching, and it's bringing out my inner drama queen.

Why don't I just pack this in? Seriously, it's becoming stupid. I'm clearly injuring myself by continuing. Stopping is both easy and sensible.

So what's it to be?

Into my mind pops a New Year run in the South Downs and another mid-run poser. Within an hour of setting off, astonishingly quickly and completely without warning, it became very foggy indeed. One minute I was lost in the scenery and solitude of a crisp January afternoon, the next I was just plain lost. I began to become melodramatic. The solitude became oppressive, the scenery irrelevant: I couldn't see any of it. I had no idea which way to turn, or how far I was from the random lay-by where I'd left the car. My in-run sense of direction is usually pretty reliable, but not, apparently, in fog. Anxiety soon became trepidation, fear, alarm, dread. It was going to get dark soon, and then I'd truly be in trouble. So what to do? Continue in the direction I was going, in the hope I would eventually arrive *somewhere* helpful, or turn back and try to retrace my steps to the car? Forward felt foolish, as I was pretty sure I was still running away from the lay-by. But it seemed equally silly to turn back towards 60 minutes of what I knew to be deserted countryside, in the slim hope that despite severely limited visibility, I might somehow recognise somewhere I'd already been.

Before I could decide, my overactive imagination kicked in and I couldn't help envisioning the worst-case scenario. I was lost in over a thousand square miles of national park. In my head, I would continue running, backwards or forwards it didn't matter, and would end up tripping over an unseen rock or hole. I would fall awkwardly, breaking an ankle, maybe both, in the process, and render myself immobile. Wearing – as I was – just a T-shirt and shorts, the sweat would turn to ice and I would soon begin to freeze. There was nobody out walking in this weather, so I probably wouldn't be found until the following morning. I began to panic. Forwards? Backwards? Stop? Fall? Freeze?

And that same panic began to grip me in Nottingham. Stop, but feel like a failure? Or continue, and possibly suffer a year-spoiling injury as a result?

Curiously, in the South Downs that day, I decided on a fourth option. I continued running, but neither forwards nor backwards. I took the next trail which turned perpendicular to the way I had been going, and tried to imagine myself running in a large loop back to where I'd started from. It didn't quite work out like that, and it was several hours and a few more moments of alarm before I eventually found my way back to the car. But now, as I continue to trudge alongside the River Trent, back towards the National Watersports Centre, towards my family and my big decision, it feels good to remember a positive outcome from a worrisome run.

And if I'm looking for further positives, I am also able to state with total certainty that whatever I choose, I'm not going to freeze today.

I'm on a boat, a beautiful wooden boat slicing through dark, calm waters. Around me sit several hundred cheerful souls also dressed in colourful kit. We're being ferried across the breathless beauty of Derwentwater in Keswick to the start of a race. A half-marathon in the fells. My first official trail run. It proves to be a seminal morning.

But by the way, how extremely cool is that? Meeting by the shores of a lake, on a glorious spring morning under blue skies, and being given your race briefing whilst scything serenely across the mirrored surface of one of England's most delightful bodies of water. Derwentwater is three miles long, a mile wide, with several small islands in the centre and surrounded on all sides by glorious, wooded hills – or fells, as they're known up here. It's the Saturday morning of the annual Keswick Mountain Festival, and nobody can remember more pleasant weather to begin the weekend.

Ironman world record holder Chrissie Wellington is also taking part in the race. We're staying in the same hotel in fact, I saw her at breakfast this morning and I'll also see her for an interview on the stage of the lakeside theatre later that afternoon. But now, as we're dropped on the opposite shore and told how to follow the route markers on the 13.1-mile run back to the festival, I know I'm unlikely to see much of her during the race itself.

And so it proves. Chrissie gallops off at the start and very few can keep pace. She's one of only two runners *not* wearing bespoke trail running shoes (I'm the other) – and I do briefly wonder if I'm making a serious, kit-related error. I also find myself pondering, as we run anti-clockwise around the enticing waters, what I've let myself in for. For instance, when the seasoned fell runners on the boat talked about the 'long, steep hills' to come, what exactly did they mean? How much longer are they, and how much steeper, than my favourite, grassy slope up to Pembroke Lodge in Richmond Park? And when they chatted about descents with a knowing look in their eye, what was that about? Also why were they forever casting surreptitious, disapproving glances at my road running shoes? And most of all, exactly how much longer than a flat half-marathon will this thing take?

I've told my family to meet me at the finish in just over an hour and a half, allowing an extra five or ten minutes for the slopes. But from what people have been saying, I get the feeling I'm being optimistic. The only thing I know for sure, as the long column of runners turns away from the shore, crosses a stream and begins to climb a fell for the first time, is that none of us will be able to keep up with the other runner in road shoes. And in that at least, I am spot on.

Chrissie did finish first – but to give you some idea of how hard and hilly the course was, her finishing time was around two hours. That's from somebody who, after a 2.4-mile swim and a hard 112-mile bike ride, can run an entire marathon, double the distance, in 2:44. I ended up crossing the line in seventh place overall, the fourth male finisher, in about 2:15. And they were two and a quarter of the most demanding yet delightful hours I have ever experienced.

I'll admit the initial hill came as a shock. The idea that we'd be doing anything other than running for the entire race had never even crossed my mind. Then we reached the first steep section of the first of many fells, and I realised that walking was the only option. And not just walking. Having slowed to a walk, I was among the overwhelming majority who climbed the severest inclines whilst awkwardly leaning forwards, with hands pushing down on knees in a bid to force the legs to straighten against the gravity of the slope. It can feel a little dispiriting at first. There are no trees at the top. It's too high.

But when you crest the hill and begin jogging again, and you lift your gaze from the ground, suddenly the sublime radiance of the Lake District unfolds before your eyes. All of England seems to lie below, and you forget about your aching thighs, and you simply sniff the unpolluted air and listen to your breathing, you enjoy the sensation of soft earth or hard rocks under your (inappropriate) shoes – and all your senses seem alive, alert, and you realise that right now, in this moment, there's nowhere else you'd rather be, and nothing else you'd rather be doing. The Dalai Lama might call it mindfulness.

A short, dark-haired woman reaches the top of that first fell alongside me, and listens for a moment as I start eulogising about how perfect it all is. She cuts me short. 'You'll need to concentrate on the way down,' she warns sternly. And then simply shoots off. She skips down the slope at startling speed. Arms wide apart, legs a blur of movement but her head stock still, eyes fixed permanently on a point about five metres ahead of her, she surges downwards, cascading over rocks and boulders as if they weren't there. I myself am on the absolute limit of control, hurtling far too fast, almost falling, but by the time I've covered a hundred metres, she's at least two hundred ahead of me. It's extraordinary. Not particularly graceful, but purposeful, resolute – and thrilling to watch. I've since heard the fell runners' mantra for descending, 'Brakes off, brain off,' and that's exactly what I'm watching disappear into the distance.

But at that moment, as she charges heroically downwards and I descend more haltingly, I become a complete convert to the trails. It's a month after the London Marathon, and I'd been idly wondering, as I frequently did, whether to recommence my quest to dip under three hours for the distance, or whether, in the words of that slightly annoying song from the film *Frozen*, to *Let It Go*.

Well, I decided as I almost tripped over a jagged bit of stone, what's two minutes and 12 seconds between friends? Not even between friends. Between myself – and myself. On the one hand, it shouldn't be too tricky to find 132 seconds over 26.2 miles. But on the other, who cares? It's not like it's the mythical *two-hour* barrier at stake here, the last great frontier yet to be crossed in athletics (some experts claim it can't humanly be achieved, while others suggest it might take another half a century to lower the current world record by the necessary few minutes). But as for me, I'm just a bloke who runs for pleasure, and the stress of trying for a marathon PB, not to mention the pressure of race day itself, would risk taking all the fun out of my running again.

So on top of that fell on that sublime spring Saturday morning, I come to a conclusion. From now on, I tell myself, forget the clock and think of yourself as a trail runner.

Rory Coleman

Running and life coach, and veteran of some 1,000 marathons and hundreds of ultras. Since starting running in 1994, he's set nine world

records and once ran all 1,275 miles from London to Lisbon to watch
England at Euro2004. Only to see them promptly lose on penalties.

I remember the day, the time, everything about my first run. It was the 5th
of January 1994 and that was my Road to Damascus moment. I'd been
thinking about that day for around six months, I just didn't know exactly
when it would be. I'd had really bad flu at Christmas and then a big
blowout in the New Year on the booze. And on January 5th I just thought,
right, I'm going to stop drinking, stop smoking, and I wanted to lose weight
because I looked in the mirror, looked at this person staring back at me
who was really overweight, and I just hated myself.

I thought runners as a rule were slim and looked athletic and healthy, so
I thought, well I'll stand on the scales, and I was 15 stone, and I thought, I'll
go for a run. I did literally 100 paces, made all the classic mistakes, set off
too quick, collapsed on the pavement with exhaustion, but I felt euphoric
because I'd found my salvation. It was a real salvation story.

When I came back and stood on the scales again, I was still 15 stone,
but it didn't matter because I knew that the next day, I'd do 200 steps,
in the dark so no one could see me, in my work clothes, leather shoes,
no specialist running gear, and the day after that, 400, and that it would
just grow and grow. At the end of the month, I'd lost 3 stone and I could
run 10 miles. In another two months' time, I did a half-marathon. And I'd
definitely found my thing.

Nowadays I coach lots of other people to run marathons; I even get paid
to run marathons.

Yesterday for instance I did a race, 26.2 miles; I plugged in my music
and I just went to a thousand different places, just trying to line up the
dominoes of life. Life's like a series of dominoes and when I run I'm trying
to get things in order. Here are some of the things I was thinking about
yesterday: one of my sons bought me a track day for Christmas and
I remembered I hadn't done anything with it, and it's May already and I'm
worried he'll think I'm awful, so that came to mind and I decided I would
buy him a track day too and then we'll go and do it together. I was also

thinking about baby Jack at home, a few months old, and wondering whether maybe I should be feeling guilty that I'm away and doing this run.

But actually, this is what I do and this is my salvation. If I ever stopped doing it, maybe I'd go back to the person I was before. It's almost like a barometer of where you are. Running is also very positive. I love that about it, rather than the hell-raising aspects of the so-and-so that I was before.

The toughest race I've ever done was 145 miles along the Grand Union Canal from Birmingham to London. The bottom of my foot came off after 70 miles. Literally. It rained, I got trench-foot and it just flapped. I didn't know much about endurance running back then and every step, it was just pain. It was just – what am I going to do? Should I finish or should I give up? As it happens I came third. I've never failed to finish any of the marathons I've ever set out to run. I'm a starter-completer.

The thing about it is that I want to do it. Nobody's forcing me to do it. The marathon I did yesterday, in Stratford, the Shakespeare Marathon, used to come past the house where I lived as a teenager and then into my twenties. I used to stand there with a pint of lager, smoking a B&H cigarette and watch the runners go by. In the early days of marathon running, they used to pass out on the lawn outside at 17 miles. We used to laugh at them. I've done that marathon ten times now and I love it.

Physically, we're absolutely designed to run, but it can help clear your head too. Lots of research has been done on this, but basically, what you do is you park things up. You park all your problems, your life, your mortgage, your overdraft, your wife, girlfriend, whatever it might be, and you put them in one place, and then for however long you're running, all you're thinking about is the next step. Literally. You're not thinking about the ones that have gone before, so if you're running a marathon at mile 10, you're not thinking about what it was like at mile 5, you're just thinking what's happening next, you're coming up to 11 miles. You're living in that moment. And in that particular moment, everything's fine. I've got to the stage now where I can just start knocking these marathons out and then I'm looking for the bigger fix, because I get longer in my own state. Things like running down a canal, 150 miles down a canal, where you get a day and a half to be in that state and actually you can't remember what it was like before you were running that race. The time's gone. All you've done, all you think about, is just being in this race.

We all have a different interpretation of it. My wife doesn't see anything when she's running, apart from what's ahead of her and the finish line. Me, I look around, I think about where I am, I run down the canal and I do some reading and find out how many litres of water there are in the locks. I go and research, I look at the tunnels and wow, 3,250 feet, that's a long tunnel. All those things become important to me. I don't know if anybody else gets what I get, but it doesn't matter because for me, it's about what I get. Running is a really personal, selfish journey that you're on. Running 100 kilometres over the Ridgeway. Fantastic, because you can't buy it. Now, if I've got endless pots of money, I can go and buy two Aston Martin DB5s. But actually I wouldn't swap my run yesterday for five Aston Martins.

◉ The Doors, *Runnin' Blue*

'OUTLAW' iRONMAN TRiATHLON, MiLE 19

'How's Andy Murray getting on?'

I'm back at Holme Pierpoint by now, back at the National Water Sports Centre where the crowds continue to enjoy the sunshine and where I'm about to make my judgement call – whether to carry on, or fall on my increasingly injured sword. Just as soon as I reach my family. And find out the latest from Wimbledon.

'He's serving for the title!' I'm told by an excitable woman in a floral dress who's watching the Centre Court drama unfold on her smartphone.

I'm sorely tempted to stop and watch over her shoulder. After all, how often do you get a chance to see a Brit winning Wimbledon? This could be History with a capital H – in as little time as it takes to fire down four aces, Murray could become the first British man since Fred Perry in 1937 to win the singles title at Wimbledon. However, if I do pause now, I know I'll never get started again, so I reluctantly turn away from the tennis and plod onwards.

Towards the family.

Towards the big decision.

Scanning the crowds on my left, I notice a large multi-coloured *Go Daddy!* banner lovingly crafted out of several huge sheets of cardboard and drawn by my wonderful children. I'm surprised I hadn't spotted it before, but as I look at it now it gives me an almighty boost. My kids grab a hand each and squeeze repeatedly in the accepted family code meaning 'I love you'. And then Caroline charmingly starts trotting alongside me in her high wedge heels and suggests she completes the race instead of me. *Please*, she implores, *I'll do it, really! Even in heels! Or bare feet! Please stop running.*

Suddenly I'm just overwhelmed with gratitude. I don't deserve to have such an awesome family, such truly terrific children and such a sensational wife. And I realise that giving up is not an option. I'd be letting everybody down. Whatever they say, they didn't come to see me *almost* complete an Ironman.

Eight miles to go then: less than 50 minutes on a good day, and not much more than an hour even at easy run pace. Today though, who knows how long? But one thing I'm suddenly sure about: I'm bloody well going to find out.

'How's Andy Murray getting on?' I ask.

'Serving for the match!' someone calls back.

'What? Again?'

'No, still.'

Blimey, I think, it must be some epic game down there.

It feels a little like I've been through something similar myself. Another tennis analogy, I was match point down, but I've made the decision to keep fighting. To refuse to bow to the seemingly inevitable and continue to believe that I might just win.

I only got lost twice on the way back to Keswick, which is pretty good, considering. Once when I was concentrating so hard on not falling over whilst descending that I missed a turning and ran all the way to the bottom of a fell before realising my mistake and having to turn around and climb halfway back up again. And once near the end, on the outskirts of a village called Portinscale, when I became over-confident, lost focus and almost ended up in the lobby of a lovely-looking lakeside hotel.

I crossed the line in seventh, but several people thought I'd won. There was such a huge gap between me and the woman in sixth that in the interim, quite a crowd had wandered into the festival grounds and congregated near the finish line. Having seen nobody else cross the line ahead of me, many assumed that I'd finished first. And later that day when I was having a cup of tea with the legendary fell runner Joss Naylor and a couple came to congratulate me on winning the half-marathon, I did absolutely nothing to correct them. Secretly, I still hope Joss reckons I won.

But I was less secretive about having fallen completely in love with what Joss does supremely, namely running in the fells. Or for me, just running in lovely, lumpy places. The notion had been creeping up on me recently: whenever I ran somewhere beautiful, new, or even just hilly, I always ran harder, freer, happier, and always finished up exhilarated. I spent the rest of the weekend, and indeed much of the following few months, telling everyone what a convert I'd become. On TV, on radio, in person. So much so that Claire Maxted, the effusive editor of *Trail Running* magazine, got to hear about it and invited me to do an interview for the next issue. And it seems I wasn't the only one being bitten by the off-road running bug.

'It's snowballing in popularity,' explains Claire when I next catch up with her, moments after she lands back in the UK having completed a six-day jungle ultra-marathon across Costa Rica (it's the sort of thing she does).

'When we started *Trail Running* magazine in 2011, it was only going to be a little leaflet, a supplement inside *Trail*. But because of the amount of interest from both readers and advertisers, we made it straight into a 148-page magazine. That first year we produced two issues, the following year it was four, and now it's six – a full magazine every two months, plus supplements.

'And the race listings section in particular has grown ridiculously quickly. We even produced an entire supplement recently called *The UK's 101 Best Trail Races*. 101! And clearly, that increase in races is to supply a demand.'

So how, I wonder, do most people get into trail running? And how did Claire?

'I've always been into the outdoors and the mountains. I used to work on *Trail*, which is a walking mag. So I was already into the trails part, I just had to get into the running part. And since I have, I've found that when I run instead of walk, I get to see more mountains in a shorter space of time! Plus I really like the idea, as a human being, of being as fit as possible. Of being able to keep going for a long time and tackle extreme terrain.

'But most people just start in their local area, in their local woods or country park. Then they might start getting a map out, reading guide books and thinking, "That bit looks interesting, I'll go and explore there and see what it's like."

'Since Keswick, I've found myself doing exactly that. Whenever I have some free time on my hands, I love nothing more than consulting a map, getting into the car and driving – driving! – to a likely looking place to have a run.

'It is, however, a big jump from running on roads, which is relatively easy – you know where you're going and you've got street lights – to seeing a footpath sign, following it on a whim, getting deep into the countryside, going off the grid.'

It is, in Claire's words: 'Simply a different sport. In fact I'd class treadmill runners and road runners in the same category, but trail running off road, getting out there, you need a new set of skills, and frequently you also need a whole new set of equipment. First of all it helps to have grippy shoes, and if you're going far you do need to carry a waterproof, food and a torch.

'To start off, people should try National Trails, which are usually very well signposted. I recently ran from Tring to Swindon, which is essentially along the Ridgeway. The signs were so amazing that I didn't need a map at all. Simply follow the footpath signs and off you go.'

And in Costa Rica, Claire discovered another reason the circulation of her magazine has been going through the roof. These days, people don't want more stuff, they want new experiences. When she comes to write about it in the relevant issue, she'll describe the Coastal Challenge she completed as 'a beguilingly beautiful adventure that will eat you for breakfast and spit out your battered bones'. And no wonder. A marathon a day for six days, with 10km of ascent – and all in 95% jungle humidity. Harder, they say, than the Western States 100-Miler where temperatures can hit 40 degrees. It costs around £2,000 to enter.

As Claire says: 'People are searching for moments in life to cherish. Rather than getting a Porsche for their 40th, they're seeking out amazing adventures. That's one of the reasons trail running has become so popular, it's more exciting than a German sports car. You'll go to unforgettable places with amazing, like-minded people and make memories that you'll treasure for life.

The camaraderie is something that appeals to a lot of people as well. Trail runners – even the elite ones – are always so friendly and keen to have a chat. Elite sportsmen and -women tend to like talking about themselves, but top trail runners want to find out about *you*.'

She mentions fells legends Naylor and Billy Bland, who were famous for waiting around after a race they'd (usually) won, and going up to other finishers and asking – and being genuinely interested in – how *they* got on. And that, it seems, is typical of trail runners. Claire experienced the same thing in Costa Rica.

'There was no separate table where the elite athletes ate. There was no arrogance, no cool set. Karl Meltzer (Speedgoat Karl, famous ultra runner and coach from Utah, USA) and Anna Frost (professional Kiwi trail runner based in Wales) both wanted to find out about my experiences every day. *How was your race, Claire?*'

Even Killian Journet, the best trail runner of all time, is apparently just a really nice bloke.

'What sets him apart is the fluidity with which he connects with the trail, looking like he's having so much fun, making ridiculous climbs look pathetically easy. And while his sheer fitness and determination surpasses everyone who's ever gone before, you'll never meet a gentler, more humble, or friendlier guy. And he's not even that big. Massive legs but tiny arms.'

There's another thing the trail running community seems particularly proud of, and that's the fact that they 'give back to the trail'.

The Marathon des Sables, the famous six-day ultra-marathon through the Moroccan Sahara, has been at the vanguard – they give something back to every village, every community they pass through. They've even built schools.

All of which is a terrific advert for swapping roads for trails. And for me it's also a great relief to know that off-road, the watch is largely irrelevant – despite the recent FKT trend (What the FKT? – it stands for Fastest Known Time for a particular trail). But I think the real rise in popularity of trail running, and certainly why I fell in love with it profoundly on top of that fell in the Lake District and why I continue to love it now, is that you'll never connect to nature in a more profound way than you do whilst running.

Allison Curbishley

Former British 400m champion, Commonwealth and European medallist. Allison has been a key member of the BBC athletics commentary team for over a decade and remains utterly passionate about the sport.

I loved the feeling of running from my very earliest memories. Anything I did had to be quick, and I absolutely had to run everywhere. Even when I became an elite athlete, even now, there's nothing better than the feeling of effortless speed powered only by yourself.

When I was four years old, in the first year of school, I vividly remember my first ever sports day. There were four years in our junior school and on sports day only the top year kids were allowed to do what they grandly called the cross-country race, which was basically just one big lap of the field. I just remember thinking that sports day shouldn't just be about running up and down a dirty, twisted, lined track that was only about 60 metres long. I was desperate to do this big, epic cross-country race. That was an aspiration from a very young age, just because I loved to be active.

And my first positive memory of running was winning that race in my final year of junior school. I did no training for it, and it's not like I was doing any structured running at the time. Neither of my parents ran, so it wasn't even instilled in me. I just remember the feeling of (a) winning, and (b) what running felt like to me, just being able to do it, being good at something. Obviously it got the competitive juices flowing even back then. I knew I was good at running, and I knew I enjoyed it.

So then during the long summer holiday between junior and senior school, my mum signed me up for a six-week, council-run athletics course – just to get me out of the house I think. This was a Monday to Friday job, 10am until 3pm, and it was down at Middlesbrough Clairville Stadium, which is now no longer there. They closed it in 2014. We did absolutely everything during that course, gave everything a try. In those days we were all obsessed with the Daley Thompson Decathlon game for the Commodore 64. You used to run by waggling the joystick from side to side as quickly as possible – and people used to get through a lot of joysticks! Anyway, during that course we were given real-life experience of every event in the decathlon, every event in athletics basically, even the pole vault. We were looked after by a couple of coaches and it was one of those guys, when my mum picked me up one afternoon, who said, 'Look, Allison has got some talent. You really want to consider bringing her down to one of the clubs.' So I began badgering and badgering my mum and dad from that day on. And from the age of 10, going on 11, I was a member of an athletics club. While I was in senior school, that's where it all became a little bit more structured. Essentially, running became my life – training every Tuesday night, training every Thursday night and racing every weekend.

But being fast, it's really something. Running at speed is amazing, and I know because I was more of a sprinter than a middle distance runner. When I started, and when I was in school, I was doing 800m, 1500m and cross country, and that gave me the base strength when I started honing in on which was my best event. My first big, national success was an English Schools victory in the 300m, which is what they made the under 15s do before moving up to 400m. So once I'd won English Schools, I knew I was the best schoolgirl at that distance and I also knew that I'd found my distance. And then it was just a case of working with the right coaches to build on my base and my talents to make me quicker and stronger.

And ironically, while more and more people are running now, competitive athletics is dropping off – not at the very top level, but at grass roots level. We used to be an iceberg-style sport: a huge base of runners and only the very best would make it to the top. Now, that base has got smaller and smaller. Meanwhile there are 5k races and 10k races every week, with thousands of people taking part. Add to that the fact that parkruns are getting bigger and bigger... But the actual competitive side of the sport, the top end of track and field, that has fewer and fewer people taking part in it. And I'm extremely worried about that because I really, desperately, don't want my sport to die. It can give you so much.

Everybody always asks, 'Do you miss it?' Well, I do miss the competition, and I miss the travelling and I do miss the people. But most of all I miss that feeling of being able to just turn it on. Almost like a racehorse. When required, you can lift yourself up and you're up onto your toes and really, it's the most natural form of exercise; running on two legs, that's what we were born to do.

🌐 Imelda May, *Road Runner*

'OUTLAW' iRONMAN TRiATHLON, MiLE 20

'Has Andy won yet?'

'YES!! Just now! He's done it!'

Wow. WOW! A British man has just won Wimbledon.

Murray has battled his demons. He's beaten the best player in the world on the biggest stage of all. He's come back from the crushing disappointment of losing the final and crying during his on-court interview, to making sure that this year, he's last in line to speak to Sue Barker. And he's looked 77 years of history full in the face and calmly overturned it.

I look down at my watch and realise I've miraculously got faster. I've just completed a mile in under eight minutes. Inexplicably, despite all the hours of hurting, I'm Popeye after a can of spinach.

Back inside a plane, back with my cousin, back for more marathon punishment – this time in Norway. This is back when road marathons were a mutual obsession. We stopped talking for a moment, paused our earnest discussion about race times, strategies and preparations, to stare out of the window and marvel at the spectacular array of islands below. The approach to Bergen airport is magnificent: hundreds of rugged islands dotted around a deep blue sea pass underneath until, all of a sudden, the runway appears and you've arrived.

At which point, straight back to our race chat.

'Are you going to try a negative split*?'

---

* Running the second half of a marathon quicker than the first.

'Hoping to, yes. How's your taper* been?'

'Nightmare. With full on maranoia† to boot.'

'Yep, me too. I think I may have over-cooked my final LSR‡.'

'I'm worried my Yassos§ have been getting slower.'

'How many tempos¶ have you done?'

'A few. But I've been doing loads of fartleks** with not enough recoveries††.'

OK, I'll stop now, but you get the idea. And we must have made quite an odd couple. Here were two Anglo-Greek men, similar-looking, both called Vassos, both talking animatedly as they disembarked from a plane and both obsessed with running a marathon in under three hours. And both convinced that Bergen, finally, was the place.

We'd been given to understand from various websites and emails that Bergen was the 'European Capital of Marathon Running' and as such, we were expecting the whole place to come to a standstill for the big race. We'd been a little surprised not to see lots of other likely looking, lycra-clad fellow runners on the flight from Heathrow, but assumed when we landed that the whole town, including the airport, would be

---

* Gradual lessening of the running load in the fortnight leading up to the marathon in a bid to arrive at the start line as fresh as possible.

† Marathon runners' (usually irrational) fear of something going wrong in the days leading up to the race, like picking up an illness or injury. Maranoia almost always incorporates lavish hypochondria, and generally drives loved ones crazy.

‡ Stands for Long Slow Run, the weekly staple of marathon training.

§ Yasso 800s, a training device invented by the famous American coach Bart Yasso. Run ten 800m repeats as fast as possible (with a 400m jogged recovery between each one), and you can convert your average 800m time, measured in minutes and seconds, into a predicted marathon finish time, in hours and minutes. It's surprisingly accurate.

¶ An uncomfortably fast, speed-improving, mid-paced run of around half an hour at lactate threshold pace, or just a little slower than the speed at which your muscles start to produce lactic acid (hurt).

** From the Swedish meaning 'speed play', this is a run that incorporates faster and slower sections.

†† Recoveries are easy runs to aid recovery from harder runs like LSRs, Yassos, tempos and fartleks. Ideally, you finish a recovery run feeling better and fresher than you did when you started it.

abuzz with excitement. We cleared customs and eagerly walked through to the arrivals hall.

Nothing. Nobody looking remotely like they were arriving to run a marathon, and nothing at all, no posters or signs or officials, to suggest that a marathon would soon take place there.

Curious.

We went in search of a taxi to the hotel. Surely the driver would know about the race tomorrow – he'd need to after all, what with all the road closures about to take effect.

'We're here for the marathon,' we explained.

The driver couldn't have looked more surprised if we'd told him we were in Norway on safari.

'But surely you know about which roads will be closing?' we insisted.

He shot a look of mild pity over his shoulder, shrugged and jabbered into his radio in rapid Norwegian.

'No marathon tomorrow,' he announced with a finality that suggested he was already tired of our charade. 'And definitely no road closures.'

Very curious.

Cue two cousins in a state of high confusion and consternation frantically looking back through our email correspondence with the man from the marathon organising committee to make sure we had the correct dates. We did. The marathon we'd flown to the small town of Bergen to run in the following morning, did indeed appear to be taking place in the small town of Bergen the following morning. Only, nobody seemed to know anything about it.

Extremely curious.

The hotel was our final hope. This was situated between the airport and the town, apparently miles from anywhere, but we'd booked it specifically at the email recommendation of organiser, Asmund, who claimed it was the official race hotel (not that we'd received any discount or anything) and extremely conveniently located for the start line.

The receptionist, predictably by now, knew nothing about any marathon taking place in Bergen that weekend. We begged him to phone around to check and he did so, but further conversations in Norwegian later, and we were still none the wiser.

Our traditional pre-marathon gluttony that night was a little subdued. We didn't know whether to tuck in with our usual abandon, to gleefully order most items on the menu in the spirit of early celebration, or whether to take it easier, fearful that the following day would be spent going for a lonely run, perhaps doing a spot of sightseeing, and otherwise killing time before our flight home.

Our mood was dark. We'd both spent three months training for this, and now it looked likely that all that hard work, all those Yassos, tempos, fartleks and LSRs, were all going to go to waste. Impossible to break three hours in a marathon that doesn't exist.

Then my cousin came up with a plan, which at least helped us enjoy our evening meal. We would, he declared, run 26.2 miles the following day whatever happened. Vassos had a top-of-the-range GPS watch which would serve as our distance guide, so even if we failed to break our PBs, at least we'd have achieved part of what we'd flown in to complete.

So bring on the Norwegian sausages, bring on the mutton meatballs, bring on the moose, the fermented trout and the cream-filled pastry pancakes for pudding. And most of all, bring on the beer (in for a penny...). To his great delight, my cousin also managed to sweet-talk the waitress into giving him her email address and the promise of a date when she came to London the following month. So despite everything, our spirits were reasonably high, his especially, as we headed to our rooms to prepare for what promised to be nothing more than a private marathon in the morning.

As it happens, when we turned up to register at the appointed time and place, a short walk along a dual carriageway and across some wasteland from the hotel, we discovered that there was indeed a proper, organised marathon happening on the outskirts of Bergen that day. It wasn't, however, a big deal. At all.

Asmund, it transpired, organised such a marathon several times every month, hence 'European Capital of Marathons'. He always used the same course – 6.55 miles along a tarmac footpath up into the hills surrounding the city, back to the start line, and repeat.

It was extremely pleasant and picturesque, but not at all conducive to a personal best. For a start, it was hilly. The Norwegian interpretation of 'quite flat' – as promised to us in the emails – and the British marathon-runners' equivalent, are markedly different things. I guess I should have known better. As I found out in Turin in 2006, *Norway is a nation of mountains and glaciers where winter sport is king*. I was at the Olympic opening ceremony that year being interviewed on Norwegian TV. The presenter had been shown around the BBC studios in Athens two years previously and had been deeply impressed.

'So how big is the BBC Radio team in Turin?'

'It's just me and a producer.'

'What?! For the Olympics?'

'We don't call these the Olympics. These are the Winter Olympics to us. We'll do well to get a medal.'

'Ah,' mused the Norwegian. 'For us it is the other way around. We say the Summer Games, but Turin, Salt Lake City, Nagano – these are the *proper* Olympics. We are a country of mountains and glaciers. Winter sport is king.'

So there you have it. In a nation of mountains and glaciers (and fjords, surely, but they weren't mentioned), 'quite flat' equals hilly. If he'd told us the course was hilly, doubtless we'd have needed ropes and crampons.

The other problem we faced, having only previously run our marathons on closed roads flanked by cheering spectators, was a certain lack of motivation. When there's nobody watching from the sidelines, nobody at all, and when you're having to dodge families out for a weekend stroll, dogs on leads, babies in buggies every few metres, it's difficult to focus on your speed and battle through the pain barrier when you need to. There were only a few dozen runners in total that morning, all spread along 6.55 miles of footpath, so you rarely came across another. And even though my cousin and I both *thought* we were digging as deep as we could, I'm not sure either of us actually did. This was confirmed the following day when we didn't feel remotely as stiff and sore as we had after previous marathon exertions. In fact we both resumed running the next afternoon.

Also, compare and contrast the happy masses lining the road at the end of (indeed throughout) the London Marathon, along with the music, the drummers, the PA system, the party atmosphere and the packed, cheering stands on the Mall, to the finishing line in Bergen: as we completed our marathons, my cousin and I, a few minutes apart, were greeted by a bored-looking bloke with his back to us pressing a button on his stopwatch and continuing to talk into his phone.

The time was disappointing too: just outside the magic three-hour mark.

Oh well, we thought on the plane home as we planned our next assault on a marathon finishing time starting with a two, at least we got to try mutton meatballs.

Jo Pavey MBE

Became the oldest female European champion in history when she won 10,000m gold in 2014 in Zurich aged almost 41, ten months after giving birth to her second child. She's also a four-time Olympian, and is currently training hard to make that five in Rio in 2016.

It wasn't obvious to me when I was a young child that I would be any good at running, because at primary school all we did was 60m or 70m sprints. I wasn't particularly good at those, but I did always keep fit, roller-skating and playing football with the lads in the street. It wasn't until I went to secondary school and I got the chance to run a bit further that I realised I was quite good. My PE teacher asked me to run two laps of a sloping grass track and she was really pleased with how I did. She recommended that I went to an athletics club, so I tried all the different events and found I really did enjoy distance running. So I joined a group that specialised in that and it went from there.

I loved the whole thing: that challenge of trying to improve my time; that I was running for me; but also, as a teenager, I enjoyed starting to travel to races in different parts of the country. I loved the aims and goals, and the social side of it too. I find that if you take pleasure in what you're doing, you keep doing it.

I still absolutely love running, and it's a real bonus to still be doing it because I thought I'd be retired at this stage in my life. I thought 2014 would be my final year, so I'm just really excited to still be out there and trying to make race plans. My massive goal is to try and make the Olympics in Rio but I'm not complacent about that; I know it's going to be tough. Still, it's exciting to keep dreaming of goals like that.

I love everything about running: the feeling of freedom, getting out into the countryside, running in beautiful places. And then I'm trying to hit targets and training; I like the challenge of that, and the challenge of the races... it's exciting. And having goals gives you some focus.

I think anyone who wants to take up running should set themselves a goal like a first 5k or 10k. You've got something you're aiming for but you can also make it sociable and go along to a running group. It doesn't have to be too serious; just enjoy your running and have something to aim for.

I love the long, slow runs too. I pick somewhere nice to run in the countryside and try to take in the scenery. It gives me a chance to gather my thoughts and think about what I'm going to do later in the day, get myself organised. Or I let my mind wander. Sometimes I imagine songs in my head. Running easily refreshes my mind really. It's quite a de-stressor, being out there and running – and when I get back in, I end up feeling better and fresher.

If you're a runner you're always a runner. I don't think I'm ever going to retire completely from running – I'm always going to run because I love it. I love the way it makes you feel good about yourself, boosts your self-esteem and it's fun to feel fit. And now that I'm a mum, it's important to show my kids that it's good to be healthy. I'm always going to run and always keep involved with running – maybe do a bit of coaching or think about getting involved with running camps. I'll definitely keep running until I'm well into old age.

🎵 Ed Sheeran, *Runaway*

'OUTLAW' iRONMAN TRiATHLON, MiLE 21

It feels good to have made a decision. To know that come what may, I'm going to finish this, or at least collapse trying. There's a new certainty, a new steeliness inside me now. No longer am I worried about doing myself a long-term injury. I've trained for *this event* for months. My inner jury has reached a verdict and I've settled on a judgement. I will carry on regardless. I'd never forgive myself if I stopped before I absolutely had to. So this is it. The pain will have to continue. The mantra that got me through my first-ever marathon comes to mind. *Just. Keep. Going.* And for some reason, I'm still getting faster. Makes no sense, but there goes another mile in well under eight minutes. Compared to what's gone before, I feel like I'm flying.

I've often thought I should join a running club. My marathon-running cousin swore by his (often brutal) Wednesday evening sessions with the Serpies in London, and would frequently cajole me to come along. I did quite fancy the sound of it, but I would always decline for the simple reason that it takes me ages to get to sleep after an evening run, especially a hard one. Like most clubs, the Serpentine Runners tend to meet in the evenings. Late nights and Breakfast Shows don't mix well.

'It's funny you say a lot of things are in the evenings, and many are, but then we also have, for example, Saturday morning hill sessions.' I'm chatting to perhaps the busiest person in Britain. Somehow I've managed to squeeze into the overflowing diary of Jennifer Bradley, chair of the UK's biggest running club (the aforementioned

Serpies), senior civil servant (head of Labour Market Strategy at the Department of Work and Pensions), running writer, baking blogger and ultra-marathoner extraordinaire. When we speak, she's recently returned from running across her second entire country (the USA; her first was France where she also conquered the fearsome Mont Blanc ultra-marathon). And she's currently, like my cousin before her, trying to persuade me that running clubs are for everybody. Even Breakfast Show sports reporters.

'For instance, that Saturday morning hill session, that's the kind of thing I would never do on my own. I would never purposely run up and down hills at speed, time and time again, until I'm feeling horrific, unless there were lots of other people doing it with me, encouraging me, trying to improve my times week on week. I think it's just about seeing the potential and not being scared.

'It's funny, the number of people who turn up the first time and have no anticipation of what it's about and then think, 'Oh, I see,' and come back again – and then get so involved that they can't imagine not having a running club as part of their life, even their social life.'

Ah yes, the social side of these clubs. This is something I've heard time and again whilst talking to people about how they first fell in love with running. Paula Radcliffe told me how it was the friends she made at Bedford and County as much as the sport itself, that kept her interested, and kept her going back. And obviously, for a runner who's new to an area, a club is an easy way to meet like-minded people and form friendships... and often more. It's often said, for instance, that the Serpentine is something of a glorified dating agency.

'Yes, we get that a lot. And we do end up with many couples getting together because it's compatible people who are choosing to do a similar thing with their evenings and weekends. Then we also have a big Christmas party, we do socials, we have a last-Wednesday-of-the-month cheese and wine event, we hold week-long training sessions abroad, all that type of thing. It's natural that you're going to get people who hook up and get together and start dating. And yeah, we have had weddings, and now there's even a whole raft of Serpentine babies. And they've all had little knitted Serpentine tops made for them. But we didn't set out to be a dating agency. We are mainly about the sport side of it, the running.'

Speaking of which, I've met several people, dozens of them, who are wary about approaching a running club, thinking they're not good enough, not fast enough, or too old. Over to Jennifer.

'The thing that really surprised me when I first joined Serpentine, and I think most running clubs fall into this bracket, is the range of abilities. Actually, it's not just for people who are good, seasoned runners. It's for everyone from beginners to women returning after pregnancy to people wanting to better their marathon time.

'And if you're nervous, it's okay just to go along with an open mind and think about how it can help you and become an enjoyable way of doing your running. Otherwise it can be quite a solitary sport.

'The bulk of our runners will be your once- or twice-a-week runners who turn up for a jog in the evening and enjoy it. Not necessarily looking to improve dramatically, maybe just focusing on a half-marathon at some point. We do focus on participation, more so than the top end. However, it's also great for the club to have some of those leading runners too, to have a good spread.

'So we have everything from beginner sessions all the way up to people who ran in the Commonwealth Games in Glasgow. We have 2,000 members. There's only ever going to be a few hundred at most who are right at the competitive top end.'

Loads of great reasons to join, and I don't know what's been stopping me. From a geographical point of view, it would probably be Barnes

Runners rather than the Serpentine or, more likely, Sheen Shufflers as they have a junior section and I think (hope) it's something my children would also enjoy. I know it would improve me as a runner. It definitely worked for Jennifer.

'Actually, it's only through joining a running club that I've got better because if I'd just kept on jogging at the same pace around Hyde Park on my own I'd probably have got bored with it. And I don't think I'd have known what to do to push myself. I've been a member ever since I started running. I came across a group of people in Hyde Park and thought "they look nice, and they're having a lot more fun running together than I am on my own" – so I just joined in. And from that, I became the first British person to run across America.'

Colin Jackson CBE

His 110m hurdles world record lasted over a decade. A multiple World Champion and Olympic medallist, his 60m world record still stands. He's now, amongst many other things, a key member of the BBC athletics commentary team.

Most probably the first time I realised I was fast was when I went to see my sister run at an event. She's five years older than me and she was running for the City of Cardiff. During her race I'm just running alongside them and I'm thinking to myself, 'Actually I'm beating the majority of these people – and I'm only three.' My sister was eight at the time. So that's when I first thought that perhaps I do have a little bit of a future in running. But you know when you're really young, you just love sport and that was me – I just loved all sports. I guess you could describe me as a competitor.

Sprint hurdles was something that came quite naturally to me. I enjoyed sprinting, I enjoyed long jumping and I enjoyed high jumping – so I thought the combination of those events could be magic. And there was something a little bit arty about hurdling, which I thoroughly revelled in – and also, I was winning the races really easily. You know when you're young and you're comfortably winning all your races, it's so much easier to get engaged with the whole event. Unfortunately I didn't grow but the hurdles did, so I had to work a lot harder to keep winning when I got older.

High hurdles is very much about a rhythm and once you get into a groove, you know brilliant things can happen. In training, you would hit this kind of rhythm that was just outstanding, and you would always want to be able to do that in competition. You knew that if you could replicate that rhythm in a big competition at some stage, you would absolutely nail a performance. I was always looking forward to a time when the conditions were going to be right and the race really mattered. When you get that kind of combination, then fireworks can happen and I was lucky enough that everything came together on that particular day at the World Championships in Stuttgart in August 1993, and I set the world record.

These days, I find it quite easy to go for a long run. That may seem quite bizarre and even as I say it, it seems very weird, because I was once measured as having 50% more fast twitch muscle than normal, and 12 times more super-fast twitch muscle. Nevertheless, I could quite comfortably complete a 10km run and I wouldn't think twice. I don't even think I would prepare for a 10km run; I would just go out there and run it. I would complete it in about 50 minutes since it's just like a nice little pace, a nice little stroll. What people may not quite understand is, to get down to around that 40 minute, 35 minute mark, you have to put some serious training in because there's a big difference. For those six miles, you need to really nail the performance. But for people who are just generally fit like myself, you could easily just stroll it in that way, 50 minutes.

I never did any longer runs when I was competing, but these days when I do, it completely clears my head. I totally disengage and I enjoy my environment and the situation that I'm in. Again it's about that rhythm. You know when you're running and you've just gotten into a lovely tempo, and when the weather is lovely like it is today, and I go out for a jog in the early morning – because that's the only time I would be brave enough to do it – that's what I do. I can clear my mind and just go.

🌐 Lionel Richie, *Running with the Night*

'OUTLAW' iRONMAN TRiATHLON, MiLE 22

One step, and then possibly the next, and then, maybe, just maybe, another.

Like a football manager giving a boring answer about not looking beyond the next match, like a tennis player refusing to see past the next round, I'm going to take this one step at a time. But actually. Literally. One step at a time. Because I have to. Because my left knee and right calf are now hurting so much that I must focus on every single footstep to gauge if I'm physically able to continue. It's an odd thing to be continuing to do something, out of choice, which goes against your every survival instinct.

Here's what's happening inside my head every half-second or so.

Left leg lands.

'Ow! That was beyond awful. The knee looks frighteningly large, and feels like a grenade has just been detonated inside it. I should pull up and get it attended to. Just wait to see what happens next time I land on...'

Right leg lifts off.

'Ow! OW! OK, forget the left knee. The right calf muscle seems to be ripping itself off the bone and disintegrating. That's going to have to improve or I'm...'

Left leg lands.

'Aaaaargh! The knee's not better then. Worse, if anything. Because that grenade now seems more like a nuclear warhead. Maybe if I try to...'

Right leg lifts off.

'Paaaaaaain!!!!'

And so on. Every single footstep.

And. *Every*. So. *Single*. On. *Footstep*.

And still around five miles left to run.

Still around fifty miles left to run. I've just completed the first mile of what will be my longest training run in the build-up to my first ultra marathon, the 100km (62 mile) Race to the Stones. But the thought doesn't especially scare me. I've never been fitter, never felt stronger, and I'm reasonably confident I can complete this without getting injured. So no, the thought of another 50 miles doesn't especially scare me.

What does alarm me a little is how fast I completed that first mile, well under seven minutes, and I'm supposed to be taking it easy. The only way I might pick up an injury is if I attempt this Long Slow Run too quickly. Trouble is, I got sidetracked during these long months of training by my old friend and training partner, the prospect of running a sub-three hour road marathon. Entirely Rory Coleman's fault with his fitness test results and fantasies of 15-minute 5ks. He probably saw a light come on in my eyes when he reeled off those outlandish figures – and even though I originally went to see him for a training plan to get me round 100km of ancient Ridgeway, even though the entire meeting was organised by the people who stage the Race to the Stones, we ended up largely ignoring the ultra and instead devising a 12-week training plan to get me round 26.2 miles as quickly as possible. So I've been doing quite a few speed sessions and power hours, probably too many – with almost certainly too little of the long stuff. I'm hoping the extra distance on the day will take care of itself if I can successfully complete this one long training route I've mapped out for myself.

The only thing is, I've set off from home and long runs always seem so much longer and harder when they're not somewhere new. There's a 22-miler following the river from Hammersmith Bridge to Kingston and back, all pancake flat, none of it difficult, but I always seem to struggle. Conversely, I once went to the south of France on a weekend jolly with pals from work. On the first morning before anyone else woke up, I covered over 30 miles in the hills above Cannes and never once felt bored or tired. The following afternoon we were in St Tropez and I set off for what I imagined would be a quick half-hour recovery. But my legs came alive as I ran through lush, shady vineyards and battled for footing on a deep sandy beach. Before I knew it, I'd been out for two hours and another 16 or 17 miles. And on the final morning, feeling a little jaded following a long and lively night before, I really did mean to run for a maximum of 30 minutes, just to sweat out the booze and loosen the legs. But again, new place syndrome, this time I ended up in a charming hilltop village called Ramatuelle and returned to St Tropez only to discover a coastal path heading out of the town the other way, past a stunning old fort and following a largely deserted stretch of coastline until it mysteriously disappeared, seemingly into the sea. By the time I returned, I'd been out for almost three hours and 20-odd miles. None of it felt hard or boring, because it was all so fresh and gorgeous and new.

But I fear this one is going to sting. Richmond Park, Bushy Park, then along the river and into the famous parks of central London, St James' Park, Green Park, and Hyde Park. All terribly green and pleasant, but also decidedly well trodden and routine. I'm beginning to think I should have driven to the South Downs and run there. Except if I had, I'd need a powerful head torch and I don't own one. Because it will be getting dark soon – and I've decided to make this an all-nighter.

I've never met anyone who's run all night, but I've heard of people who have and it seems right up my street: an enchanting mix of unusual, romantic, soulful and bonkers. I set off as the rest of the world heads home after a long day's work and suddenly realise that my excess speed for the first mile is actually down to excitement. This is bracing, invigorating. The rush hour traffic is worse than usual, and I feel liberated as I gallop along, not constrained by cars, traffic lights, roadworks or deadlines. It's mid-June and the perfect weather for running, cloudless and still, warm but not hot. There are others on the towpath too, lots of them taking advantage of the long summer evening – commuters on bicycles, couples out for an evening stroll, dog-walkers, pram-pushers and of course fellow runners.

My pace has slowed now, in keeping with my need to avoid injury, and as someone overtakes me I have to fight down the urge to race him. Normally I'd be going faster than that, I think. But pride has no place in an all-night run. Not that sort of pride anyway, not the corrosive kind.

Over the next hour or two, as the cars thin out on the roads, I see fewer and fewer people on the pavements and paths. I suddenly decide I no longer want to be running in deserted suburban parks. The night is an ideal time for an urban adventure. I'm in Richmond Park by now, the sky is finally darkening, and I've not seen another human being for around half an hour. Despite how close I am to millions of people, the apparent solitude begins to wear on me and I turn out of the park, ripping up my carefully crafted plan in the process, and start heading northeast alongside the still-busy A3 towards town.

This feels better, my legs get a new lease of life and my heart soars despite the fact I've swapped nature for noise, trees for traffic, beauty for buildings. It feels a little weird, plodding alongside a dual carriageway and heading for one of the busiest cities in the world to continue my run. Good weird? I've not decided yet. Different though, definitely different.

I soon find myself in the Wandsworth one-way system, still gridlocked as people start falling out of pubs, bars and restaurants. Many of them look quizzically at the guy who's clearly opted for this less conventional way to spend his Thursday evening. But I'm only alongside them for a moment as I head onwards into Clapham, which is also surprisingly busy. I realise I'm becoming a bit of a nuisance running down the pavement of a busy high street, because no-one coming out of a bar expects people to be travelling at anything more than walking pace at this time of night.

I remember that my wife used to live round here, so I resolve to detour round each of the four flats she rented before we got married, as a sort of pilgrimage to old times' sake. Except I get lost looking for the first of them and end up in Brixton, not Battersea as I'd hoped. And if I thought the nightlife in Clapham was spirited, it's nothing compared to busy, bustling Brixton. I jog past a nightclub called the Dogstar just as a loud group of girls leaves and a larger group of lads turns to go in. A few years ago, I'd have been one of those boys, energised by booze and giving the running bloke a similarly sardonic stare.

I turn northwards, heading for the Thames via the Oval cricket ground and Westminster Bridge. Everything seems much quieter now, the pavements are thinning out and people are heading home, even the revellers. Except for a few couples and tourists out strolling, the riverside is obligingly peaceful, and there's nothing to draw my attention away from the world's greatest cityscape – Houses of Parliament, Southbank, Tate Modern and London Eye all viewed over calm water at night. The old and the new, perfectly in tune. The draw of history is even stronger here than it was that day on the Isle of Wight, when I felt a powerful connection to runners of previous generations, previous centuries, who'd doubtless been struck by the same sense of splendour as they reached the top of a Down and gloried in the sight of the island tapering towards the Needles. I wonder if Wordsworth had a touch of the night runner about him when he wrote *Composed Upon Westminster Bridge*:

> *Earth hath not anything to show more fair:*
> *Dull would he be of soul who could pass by*
> *A sight so touching in its majesty:*
> *This City now doth, like a garment, wear*
> *The beauty of the morning; silent, bare...*

It was early morning when Wordsworth wrote those evocative lines 200 years ago, and it's very early morning now, almost 2am as I head past Downing Street into Trafalgar Square, Covent Garden and Soho. This being the party capital of the capital (as it were) there are still quite a few people on the streets and I find I'm enjoying the incredulous looks

I receive as I dodge between bouncers and partygoers. It's then that I realise I'm not remotely exhausted despite the fact I've been running for almost five hours. In my legs, that is. My legs feel relatively fresh and loose, but my head could definitely do with a strong coffee to keep it ticking over. And having lived in the middle of Soho for over a year in my twenties, I know exactly where to get one. Bar Italia is a London institution: it's been going since the 1940s, open 22 hours a day (they only close between 5am and 7am) and their coffee is top banana. There's often a queue, even in the middle of the night, but tonight I'm lucky and get served immediately. So I down a quick double espresso at the bar, wolf down a few biscuits – and feel ready to tackle the rest of the night.

But I also suddenly crave some solitude, so head north for Regent's Park and Primrose Hill. As I run through the largely empty streets and into the deserted parks, it feels like I've put the city to bed, all tucked up and cosy, whilst I continue to patrol outside.

I had feared that running alone in an empty park at night might be a touch scary, or at the very least spooky. But it turns out London's copious green spaces are glorious places to be in the early hours, and I happily while away an hour or two, just thinking, clearing the head of clutter, and all the while I hardly see another soul even though I'm right in the centre of a city of over eight million.

Before I know it, it starts getting light again and just as it does, I also start feeling drowsy. The caffeine has long since worn off. I consider racing back to Bar Italia for another before it closes, but change my mind. Only another hour or so to go now, so I perk myself up with a Snickers bar and some hill repeats – a dozen times up and down the face of Primrose Hill. Whether it's the chocolate, the intervals, or a combination of both I don't know, but it works. I feel newly energised. There are others runners about by now, and suddenly I'm just normal again, just another bloke stretching his legs before work. But to me, it feels like I've been calmly watching over everyone, like a parent, waiting for the city to wake.

I'd also been a little concerned about what state I'd be in when I arrived at New Broadcasting House for the Friday morning Breakfast Show, but again, I needn't have. I'm fine. I'm also rather proud of myself. I have no idea how far I've gone, but I've just run through the night for the first time. And as I swipe into the building and head for a much-needed shower, I feel sure it won't be the last.

Graham Albans

Senior Producer on the Chris Evans Breakfast Show on BBC Radio 2. He hadn't run a single step until six months ago, but he's now joined a running club, absolutely loves the way it makes him feel, has lost loads of weight and has even persuaded friends and family to take up running.

I think running is one of the only sports where you're not competing against... well for me I'm not competing against other people, I'm only competing against myself. It's that realisation that I'm never going to win a race, I'm never going to come first. But what I can do is continually try to beat myself and compete against myself and continually better myself.

The reason the whole thing started for me in the first place wasn't because I wanted to get into a sport – I've never been into sport – or even that I wanted get into running particularly. It's that I wanted to lose some weight and be healthier. So now I'm competing against the scales as well. Every couple of weeks I'm looking at the scales and trying to beat my target weight or beat my target time at a parkrun or beat my distance in a training run in the middle of the week.

My first parkrun was in February 2014. I couldn't finish it. It was a cold morning and I had a bit of a cold but I think I was sort of using that as an excuse. I just couldn't get air into my lungs and I felt horrible. I felt like a failure because I couldn't even make it round one lap, I walked a bit, carried on running, but halfway round the second lap I literally had to stop and walk back to the car. My legs had no more go in them. It just felt rubbish, especially as I was right next to my friend Phil who's a super runner and breezes through these things in 18 minutes. The maximum I had done up until that point was four kilometres and I couldn't finish my first 5k parkrun, which felt lousy.

Now my PB at parkrun is just over twenty minutes. And I absolutely love it.

Some friends have persuaded me to think about longer runs. I would have thought it would be completely unachievable but downloaded some basic training plans for a half-marathon. You think, 'I'm never going to get into these longer distances', but you can if you follow a plan and don't just be lazy. Each week my weight came down and down and my fastest times came down and down and my distances went up and up and up.

Now I'm six months into a very short but very enjoyable running life. You can't keep me off the roads. I have to remind myself that I need to take a rest day every now and again because when I go a day without putting my trainers on it doesn't feel right. I feel really sluggish and lazy on the days that I don't do it.

I feel totally better physically and mentally. I sleep better when I'm asleep; I'm more awake when I'm awake. I feel better in the clothes that didn't used to fit me and now do. I just feel more vibrant and I concentrate better. It feels good to have a physical hobby as well, something outside of work that I can get into and I've made friends through.

Running is another element to my life which is a massive, positive thing. And directly because of me starting to run, my mum and dad have both laced up their trainers again (my dad used to run half-marathons but gave up years ago). And friends have been getting out running for a few miles just because I've been buzzing about it. A year ago Vassos was the only runner on the breakfast show. Now all of us have achieved at least a half-marathon, and Chris himself secretly ran the full London Marathon! It's a ripple effect. And it's all good.

🌐 Jay-Z, *Run This Town*

'OUTLAW' iRONMAN TRiATHLON, MiLE 23

It's been cathartic, this.

Despite the fact that I'm hobbling round this marathon much slower (two hours slower) than anticipated, and despite the fact that I'm likely to be injured for some time, I begin to sense that it's all been worthwhile. Because the whole point of this was to challenge myself, to dig deep and see what was in the well. And thanks to my various injuries and nutrition fiascos, I'm certainly doing just that.

In fact nothing I've done before or since, not running through the night or attempting an ill-prepared 100km cross country in worn-out shoes, nothing has hurt or tested me as much as this.

I realise that despite everything, I've already sort of won. Even with four miles to go. I've tested myself to my limits, and come through. A clever man once gave me some advice. You should, he said, try to get out of your comfort zone as frequently as possible, ideally every day. That way your comfort zone expands and you become more and more accomplished as a human being.

Well, today I've gone way, way, WAY out of my comfort zone. And if I can get through another four miles, I will feel I've truly grown.

But that's still a big if.

Text message received. From Coleman, Rory:

So how did the Kent Roadrunner go?

Gulp. Best get this over with.

Thanks for remembering Rory. Really nice event, super people, but I had a shocker. 3:15. No idea why, I looked back through my training and it was practically perfect.

And it was. As I've mentioned, I was meant to be training for my first ultra-marathon, but got sidetracked by the idea of running a fast marathon on the road. Or more specifically, on the 2.5km track of the Cyclopark near Gravesend in Kent. Seventeen laps of it.

I was unusually nervous the night before the race, and indeed the night before that, on marathon eve eve, and opted not to join the other dozen or so dads on my street for our last-Thursday-of-the-month meeting in the local pub. These are usually reasonably tame affairs, but just in case...

The reason I was nervous is that by and large, I'd followed Rory's training plan to the letter. Weekly Power Hours that left my calves aching for days. Hill sessions. Speed sessions. Long runs, longer than prescribed. Weight sessions in the gym. Daily core exercises... I'd done it all. And the previous week, when Rory had come into Radio 2 for a chat and I'd told him how quickly I was running, he confidently predicted my marathon time would be 2:49 to 2:54. Mind you, he added, it's on the undulating side, that Cyclopark, so watch out for that.

Undulating? Nobody had mentioned anything about undulating. Still – I was injury-free, my training all but completed, an expert was forecasting a fast time on a course he knows – I could approach my taper with confidence.

I even printed out a cut-out-and-wear wristband from the Roadrunner website telling me how fast I should run each lap if I wanted to finish in 2:50. I chickened out of wearing it at the last minute, thinking it might look a little pathetic amongst all the Garmins. I was, I believed, in even better shape than I had been the previous autumn when my training times suggested I was about to run a sub-3 Bournemouth marathon. I pulled out the day before the race when my baby daughter went into hospital. She came out the following Friday, and the morning after that I annihilated my 5k PB – a combination, I think, of an extra week's taper, and a monumental release of tension.

But on the evening before the Kent Roadrunner, the idea that I wouldn't coax my marathon PB into starting with a 2 was preposterous.

Only two minutes and 12 seconds to shave off, and I felt at least 15 minutes faster than I ever had before. I was nervous, but excited. The perfect combination.

Nothing on the morning of the race suggested it wasn't going to go well, and the first few laps were magical. But then I mysteriously felt myself slowing down. Each lap was increasingly sluggish, and though I was still on course to break three hours at half way, I knew I didn't have it in me. For a long moment, perhaps a minute or so, I considered allowing my inner eight-year-old to take control and petulantly stop running altogether. *If I'm not going to break three hours, I may as well give up!*

But that's hardly the point of this running lark, is it? If marathons teach you anything – and they do – then lesson one is surely not to give up when the going gets tough. Marathon 101: just keep going. So instead of scowling my way to the finish line, I decided to enjoy the day for what it was. Which was a celebration of marathon running all the way round the track. The advantage of a multi-circuit event is you get to chat to the same people in the crowd (hello, Tracey, with the big bowl of giant Jelly Babies) every time you run past them, and the supporters get to see lots of their loved ones (and thank you Katie's mum and dad for letting me leave those gels on your table).

In the same lap as I fell out of love with running (*wasted months of training, what's the point?!*), I fell back in love with it twice over. The event felt like a full-fat parkrun – all that positivity, all that exertion and all that determination, eight and a half times over (distance-wise, at any rate). So in a sense I was pleased to have struggled, because it reminded me that running is about so much more than race times.

Plus, I was overlooking a somewhat basic error I'd made in the days leading up to the race. I may not have gone to the pub, but I did accidentally overtrain. I went to a treadmill to make sure I ran 5km at exactly race pace *and no quicker*. But I ended up knocking out an hour-long, 15km thrash on a 3.5% incline. My reasoning, which is faulty at the best of times and completely mangled whilst exercising, had gone something like: *this feels too slow, perhaps I should push the pace so it seems easier on race day, yes I'll do that but also, I should increase the incline so it replicates the difficulty of running outdoors and why don't I push that up to double what it needs to be, so again it feels easier on Saturday, and why don't I triple the distance too, just because...* Honestly, I've done dozens of these things, yet the way I went about this marathon, you'd think I was a complete novice. Rory certainly thought so, as his texts kept coming.

RC: Yikes. That's disappointing as the course is OK for times. Did you set off too quickly?
VA: Not really. Just nothing in legs.

RC: Did you carbo load? Gels?
VA: Yep. Yep.

RC: And the week before you took it easy?
VA: I may have overdone it on the treadmill on Wednesday as calves were sore Thursday and Friday.

RC: Instead of the three easy miles in your plan?
VA: Ah.

RC: You know it's dangerous for you to think. All that training gets wasted otherwise. Just follow Uncle Rory's plan as he knows best.

'Uncle Rory' went on to suggest I entered another marathon a fortnight later, taper properly, and see what I could achieve. Only I was busy for the next three weekends, and after that it was getting dangerously close to the 100km Race to the Stones and I didn't want to risk picking up a niggle. I'd meant to run the magnificent Giants Head marathon too, but a last-minute, un-turn-downable job offer put paid to that. So I decided to put things right where I'd got things wrong. Back on the treadmill in the gym. A 2% incline this time to compensate for lack of wind resistance, set speed at 14.5kph (9mph), and run 26.2 miles. And it was ridiculously straightforward. I know it doesn't count as an official marathon PB, but I also know, finally, *finally*, that it really doesn't matter. I needn't have worried for all those years about the 2 mins 12 seconds.

As I realised my sub-three ambition (which I later repeated outside), I understood that while it's important to have goals, it's equally important not to let them dominate to such an extent that you stop enjoying your running.

Although having said that, I'm pretty sure I could go quicker...

Richard Nerurkar MBE

British marathon runner and Olympian. Won the 1993 World Cup marathon and Hamburg marathon. Finished 5th in the 1996 Olympic marathon in Atlanta. Author of the invaluable training aid Marathon Running: From Beginner to Elite.

I started running competitively at school when I was nine years old. It started in the sports lesson – there was just a race around the park across the road from the school I went to. It was one lap around the park and I won it. I think I broke the record. It was those early days of running at school which made me realise that this was something I liked doing and was good at.

From the start I enjoyed that feeling you get when you're running, that feeling of being fit and being able to exercise in a way that you can take pleasure in, that isn't a struggle. I still love that, along with the feeling running gives you afterwards. I also like the direct competitive side of it (though I'm now no longer competing really, so I'm more competitive with myself; that's great too). In years gone by I relished the challenge to be as good as I could possibly be, and to compete against other people.

My favourite runs were probably the ones we used to do in Ethiopia, in Addis Ababa. We lived there for ten years and my wife and I still go back frequently. I can think of countless places where I've run all over the world, and even though some of them are simply amazing, there was something very, very special – and there continues to be something very, very special – about running in the early morning hours in the forests of Addis Ababa. In some ways running doesn't get much better than that.

The way I read it, the boom in running happened in the early 1980s and then plateaued for about ten years until about the mid-90s. At that time, certainly in Britain due to the success of the London Marathon, mass participation running really took off. That was partly driven by the charities too, seeing that it was a great opportunity to raise funds and that runners wanted to run for good causes.

Of course all of that was superb and I think it's great that running continues to thrive as a sport. I'm amazed that it's still a boom sport really, but delighted by it too. Running is clearly not a fad that has come and gone. It's something that is still hugely popular, both in Britain and across the world. It still remains an incredibly accessible sport – it's very cheap and it's something that everyone can do at almost any stage in life. I'm now in my fifties and I see people who take up the sport in their forties and fifties and they never look back. I think that's wonderful.

◉ Bryan Adams, *Run To You*

'OUTLAW' IRONMAN TRIATHLON, MILE 24

I'm close enough to the finish to sense that I'm going to enjoy it when I get there. But I'm in way too much pain to enjoy it yet. My knee remains in agony every time I land on it, while my calf is still shrieking in protest too. Just three miles to go, but it feels like an awfully long way. I tell myself that it's the same distance as I run most Saturday mornings with the kids, and try to remember my daughter's first parkrun, back when running was a real struggle for her.

It's tough when you're a kid; your sense of time hasn't fully developed so all the bad stuff, like double maths or your first 5k, seems it will go on, *like forever!* I try to put myself in her (then) eight-year-old shoes and imagine how she must have felt. She was out of breath, and her ankle hurt, and she got a stitch, and then another. She had one brief walking break at half way, and it took a lot out of her to continue running after that. Those three miles back then would have felt like a seriously long way. And these three miles today feel like a seriously long way.

So there you go, if nothing else, parental empathy.

My dad never ran, but his brother – my Uncle Tony – did. He was a sprinter, and a pretty good one by all accounts. An Oxford Blue, he still holds his secondary school record for the 100 and 200 yards. It's his son who travels round Europe with me running marathons. So I do wish Uncle Tony would stop forwarding me articles with titles like 'Too Much Exercise May Be Harmful To Your Health'. I know we journalists love a headline, but still. They worry me. And now, having just enjoyed a late breakfast with one of the world's leading experts in this field, those articles also slightly annoy me. Because as I've just discovered, they're basically wrong.

'The key thing is this...' says Dr Greg Whyte, an Olympian turned sports physiology professor, as he reaches for the croissants. It's Greg who trained Eddie Izzard to run 43 marathons in 51 days for Comic Relief, Greg who helped Davina McCall run, swim and cycle 500 miles from Edinburgh to London for Sport Relief, and Greg who's also helped James Cracknell, John Bishop, Cheryl Cole, Dermot O'Leary and others complete their charity challenges and raise over £17 million in total. He also travels the world giving keynote speeches on this exact subject. He definitely knows what he's talking about.

'...As soon as you stop being sedentary and start becoming active, lots of positive things happen, and your whole health improves. You reduce the risk of cardiovascular disease, metabolic syndrome, type 2 diabetes; you reduce your risk of cancer, peripheral vascular disease, depression, low self-esteem. And the more you do, the better that response, the better you become.

'The greatest gains are made at the early stage, as you first start exercising, and then the law of diminishing returns kicks in – you have to do more and more exercise to experience the same health gains. Beyond 150 minutes a week, which is the World Health Organisation guideline for how much exercise to do, you've got to work very hard indeed to get further gains.'

However, that article from Uncle Tony suggests there must be a point where the graph starts to turn down again. So can you do so much exercise that instead of getting positive gain, you actually start to deteriorate? Or, as Greg puts it, 'where the law of diminishing returns starts to become pathophysiologic.' As Director of Research for the

British Olympic Association for six years, he spent – and indeed still does spend – a lot of his time talking about this.

'We are the best endurance animal of any species on the planet. As persistent hunters on the African plains we would chase our prey for days on end, and the one thing that differentiates us from any other species is our ability to thermo-regulate. We are truly great sweaters. Dogs don't sweat, horses have real trouble thermo-regulating. That's what makes us such a tremendous endurance animal. We're built for it.

'With running, it's what's called linear endurance. You're repeating the same activity over and over and over again. What that does is strengthen muscles, strengthen bones and strengthen joints. So what you find is that endurance athletes are incredibly strong and stable. Running doesn't bring on osteoarthritis. In fact you prescribe exercise when you get it. The only thing that works for the osteoarthritic patients I look after, the *only thing that works*, is exercise.'

Humans being 'built for running' is also the mantra of the barefoot runner. The increased prevalence of running injuries, they'll tell you, only came about with the advent of the extravagantly cushioned shoe. Back in the day, the argument goes, back before cars and bikes and even horses, back when humans had to run to get places, they did so without cushioned soles and anti-pronation support systems. Biomechanically, we're born to run a certain way, and our running shoes are hindering that, hence all the injuries. So more and more people have decided to ditch traditional trainers and either run with minimal cushioning like the Nike Free, or in basically no footwear at all, like the Vibram FiveFingers (which is not so much a shoe as a thin rubber casing for the foot with a flexible sole and visible individual sections for the toes. It looks kooky, but also kind of cool).

As it happens, I wholeheartedly agree with the barefoot theory but don't have the courage to change out of my trusty Asics. Firstly, because if it ain't broke don't fix it. And also, I don't want to have to spend up to a year making the transition. And make no mistake: swapping my Gel Cumulus for some FiveFingers would basically involve re-learning how to run. And that would mean another trip to Mike Antoniades from Mile Four, the founder of The Running School who helps people improve their technique to reduce the risk of injury. He has lots to say about the (both relatively new, and also of course ancient) act of barefoot running.

'Remember, it's a choice, not a technique. People like the idea of running barefoot because they believe it's how we were meant to run. And in the summer, when they walk on the grass, it's a great feeling because we have sensors on the bottom of our feet.

'It's correct that the huge increase in running-related injuries started with the advent of cushioned shoes. And now the manufacturers are taking a right old beating about it. But if you look at their market, and if you look at supply and demand and profitability, those companies would have considered that their biggest market was urban runners. And how do urban runners run? Heel to toe. So they simply stuck a big cushion on the back of the shoes to stop urban runners getting injured.

'We know that the most efficient way of landing is on the forefoot. But if you just swap your shoes and change the way that you land without changing the rest of your technique, all you're doing is transferring more pressure to a different point.

'The other thing that people forget is that to change the way you land can sometimes take 12 months. Because you are adjusting to the new forces, transferring the stress from heel to toe to the forefoot – the calf and Achilles overwork. So a lot of people who switch get even more serious injuries. It's definitely not for everyone, and recreational runners in particular should think twice.'

And while they do that, back to breakfast with Greg. As he was saying, far from causing bone or joint problems, running long distances actually helps. I'll ask him about the thorny issue of the heart in a moment, but is there *anything* health-related that endurance sport exacerbates?

'With excessive exercise you do compromise immune function. Initially it helps though – so when you first start running, you'll get fewer colds. But athletes who do exorbitant amounts of training do get upper respiratory tract infections more frequently. And that can evolve into what we now call Unexplained Underperformance Syndrome (UPS). Many people would put the colds and the UPS at the foot of increased physical activity, of overtraining. But we now know it's probably nothing to do with the exercise. It's actually more about the compound effect of other stressors in life – exams, splitting up with a girlfriend, money or job worries, that sort of thing. Life is about balance, and in this case it's about stress and recovery. Effectively when you add these large social stressors on top of extreme training, the balance becomes lopsided and the recovery is not great enough to cope with the stress. Therefore the athlete can fall into this downward spiral of immune disruption and underperformance.'

As he's speaking, I both inwardly berate myself for never having heard of UPS, and then blame it for every disappointing race I've ever run. That time I failed to break three hours in Kent? UPS. The 10k race in Greenwich when I couldn't get inside 40 minutes? UPS. That New Year's Day half-marathon when I went way over an hour and a half? Actually, that was more likely to be the hangover.

A waitress approaches and warns us breakfast service is finishing and she'll soon need the table back for lunch. So I can't put it off any longer, the long-term, low-level worry I was doing my best to ignore despite the best efforts of Uncle Tony. It was going to have to find a voice. Can running ultra-marathons damage the heart? The latest reports say 'yes'; it's what my uncle emailed me about most recently.

Greg is definitely the man to ask.

'I've published sixty papers on this. In almost all cases, almost all runners, including those that do the occasional marathon, there's absolutely no evidence that it can damage the heart. As we move towards the world of the ultra-endurance nutter, there is a certain suggestion that it might be problematic in individuals who have a particular susceptibility.

'But one of the guys I studied, he'd done 656 marathons and 256 ultras, he's at one very extreme end of the spectrum. Downstream from that, for anybody else basically, the odds are pretty good. Of course it makes headlines when somebody dies during a big city marathon, but there's always a reason. So unless you have pre-existing underlying cardiovascular disease, running is very positive and will improve the health of your heart.'

Thanks Greg, I'll take that. There's a tiny risk of exacerbating a heart problem you had anyway, but an overwhelming probability that you're doing your heart the power of good. I might just have to redirect Uncle Tony's next email to the junk folder.

Greg Whyte OBE

Former Olympian, World and European Championship medallist. Now an acclaimed sports scientist who's helped train celebrities to raise almost £20m for Comic Relief and Sports Relief through various extraordinary challenges.

I started off as a swimmer. As any swimmer will tell you, swimmers hate running and swimmers are no good at running. Ask a swimmer to run; it's the funniest thing you'll ever see. It's classic.

So yes, I started off as a swimmer when I was six, and in those days you could compete when you were six. Even at that age I was doing county championships, and soon onto nationals. Then at the Olympic Games in 1976, when I was nine, there was a huge scandal involving modern pentathlon [swimming, shooting, equestrian, fencing and running]. A guy called Jim Fox was captain of the Great Britain team, and he caught a Russian, Boris Onishchenko, cheating in the fencing. Disonishchenko, as he was called in the papers, had modified his épée so he could register a hit without actually touching his opponent. The Soviets were thrown out and Britain went on to win gold. This was right at the height of the Cold War so it was a global story and pentathlon became a reasonably high-profile sport.

At that time, I began dabbling. That's when I started running, really, because first it was biathlons, run–swim biathlons. Then you added shooting – triathlon – and then into tetrathlon with the fencing. The equestrian came last.

As a swimmer, my first run was misery, just misery. Think about it – swimmers have upper body strength, upper body power. And the lower body, the legs, you don't really need them for swimming. You just don't need any lower body. So running was always a struggle, and I mean mentally as much as physically. I was a great swimmer and I wasn't a great runner, so the people I would mow down in the pool, I was unable to catch on the track.

At school I was one of those kids, I guess you'd expect, who was in every team, and that included cross country. Every kid, even the good runners, hated cross country because it was always in winter and it always seemed to be snowing or raining – and muddy. The enduring image I have from those races is thinking, 'You know what? I am built for swimming.' That's why I spent such a long time, and a huge amount of work, on improving my running, trying to bring the run up to the level of the swim.

The reason I learned to love running, and still do, is because it is about me; it's not necessarily about anybody else. And I'm running against myself. I'm not running against other people. Let's say you do the London Marathon: there are 36,000 other people in the race. Unless you cross the line first in two hours, three minutes, you're not going to win the race. So what that means is it's almost like the pressure is off. You can just run your race and you've got a target time that is specific to you and nobody else.

I never listen to music. When I first started doing sport, the best that you could get was the Sony Walkman. If you can think back and remember, it was big and yellow and they claimed it was waterproof... Well, first of all the batteries used to run out really quickly, but also, when you're running along, it used to jar the music so you couldn't listen to anything. So I think I grew up and trained not listening to music and now I just can't. If I'm in the gym doing a session and the music's on, that's fine.

But I just love to get out on the road, in the park; I love being in the mountains running. Just me, just me and the road, me and the grass, and I just run through the week in my mind, run through what's going on, run through my plans. There's almost a freedom to it. I can't answer emails when I'm running. It's brilliant.

And having just completed the Marathon des Sables, I'm now a swimmer who loves running.

◉ Beyoncé, *Run the World*

'OUTLAW' iRONMAN TRiATHLON, MiLE 25

Grumpy emoji. I may be close enough to the finish, probably for the first time all day, to be able to practically guarantee that I'll make it. But still, grumpy emoji. And if there is one, furious, steam coming out of non-existent ears emoji as well. Because I've just had a clear vision of the summer that lies ahead of me, and there's not much running involved.

It's been there as a constant, underlying concern throughout, the fact that I could well be doing myself some proper damage by continuing to run through this pain. But now that the finishing line is so close, that worry has crystallised into fact. *Of course* I'm giving myself an injury. Of *course* I won't be able to run for a while. What have I been *thinking*?

As it turned out, I did get properly injured, my calf took weeks to recover and my knee never has. But the rest of the summer was surprisingly pleasant – I did lots of swimming, much of it in open water, which was (and is) completely ace. It was several months before I was able to run again. And even years later, that left knee still hurts most days, appallingly so if I twist or jar it. But I can usually now run on it – and that's essentially all I ask of it.

So two miles to go, grumpy emoji, as well as the furious emoji with the steam. But yes, also happy emoji and relieved emoji with a great big grin because there are only two miles to go. Fifteen minutes or so. And as for any lasting injuries I'm self-inflicting – well, I'll deal with them later.

Which is exactly what I did. And still am.

'It's like buying expensive speakers.'

I'm running slowly, carefully, contentedly, through a vast, undulating cornfield somewhere in Oxfordshire, Berkshire or Wiltshire (it's a little hard to tell) and chatting amiably to somebody I've just met called Harry, a property developer and father of three from Camberwell in South London. The speaker analogy is his. I don't understand it.

'This ultra-marathon we're running, and I've done a few before, it's like buying expensive speakers. At low volume you can't tell the difference. So if you want to find out about yourself, really see what you're made of, you need it noisy. A short race is too quiet. But 100km is loud.'

Great analogy, I tell him.

'You're bound to hear better,' replies Harry.

I tell him I seriously doubt it, though as it happens I do.

For the time being, however, I look forward to turning up the volume in a few hours' time. In fact I've been looking forward to today, to my first ultra, for months. It's the 100km Race to the Stones, 62 miles along the ancient Ridgeway, apparently the oldest path in Britain, ending at a 5,000-year-old stone circle in Avebury, just south of Swindon. The path wends its way from the Chilterns to the Wessex Downs through sun-speckled beech woods, abundant wildflower meadows and fields of swaying wheat. Chalky trails and woodland tracks pass Neolithic burial chambers, Bronze Age hill forts and the mammoth prehistoric figure of the White Horse, carved white into the lush green hill at Uffington. Traces of a hundred generations.

Super-coach Rory Coleman is also running and joins in the chat, warning Harry and me that we're going too quickly and may pay for the pace later in the race. Caroline from Ireland wonders loudly what on earth she could have been thinking when she decided to enter. Somebody else pipes up that 'the darkness' as he calls it tends to descend somewhere between miles 30 and 35, and when it comes, lasts for about an hour before lifting. Remember that, he says, it does lift.

These are the early stages of my ultra-marathon debut, and I'm enjoying the fact that it all feels so relaxed. You're not constantly under pressure like you are in a marathon; you're not on your lactate threshold for the entire race, checking your watch, calculating your speed, fretting that miles are ticking by too slowly for you to achieve a PB. You can relax, breathe, look up, enjoy the scenery, chat, natter and make new friends. Unless, that is, you're at the front trying to win the thing or break the course record – and I know a few who are. I dread to think what horrors they go through for such an extended period. It's bad enough running whilst stressing for 26 miles and three hours. What must it be like for 62 miles and ten hours?

No such worries for me or my new buddies. There's airy talk about the possibility of finishing in under 12 hours, that apparently being a decent benchmark for this event. But it's more a curiosity – *I wonder if I'll break 12 hours* – than an actual target. So we plod onwards, at blissfully low intensity so nobody's out of breath and chatting is easy. The mini-targets are the aid stations, strategically placed every six miles or so along the route, each offering a perfect array of sugary granola bars, deliciously salty crisps, chocolate, flapjacks, water, tea, coffee, flat cola and best of all, purple squash. I fall in love with the purple squash, especially with added salt. Later in the race, at aid station seven or eight when I'm ever so slightly delirious, I'll loudly proclaim undying love to the purple squash and threaten to propose to it. I would have done so too, if I'd been physically able to get down on one knee after 50-odd miles of hilly running.

The company changes frequently as some runners linger for longer at the aid stations, or stop for random walking breaks; others pause to rummage in rucksacks and others still surge ahead. So as Rory pops to the loo, Caroline stops to stretch and Harry takes five to find some antacid tablets (his 'secret weapons'), I find myself running on my own for the first time. It's actually rather pleasant to find yourself almost 20 miles into a race, and not be hurting or struggling or gasping for breath. To be jogging along well within your comfort zone and simply enjoying the spectacular scenery. I pass through three villages each of which are utterly beautiful and I decide I must move there at once.

In one, there's a riverside pub looking so inviting and gorgeous it takes a surprisingly large amount of willpower to restrain myself from popping in for a pint.

The only nagging concern is that I'm running too slowly – it feels odd to be trundling along at this pace. But, as I keep reminding myself, my only concern is *not* a concern today: time is gloriously irrelevant.

Past full marathon distance, and I'm still feeling strong. I start chatting to someone who's been running nearby for the past mile or two. It turns out he's called Tim, lives in Winchester with his fiancée, and is also attempting his first ultra. We chat amiably for a few miles, and I'm impressed to discover that Tim has won, actually won, his local parkrun more often than he hasn't (the best I've managed is fourth). He's run five marathons before today but never as stand-alone races, always at the end of long triathlons. His best marathon time is 3:30, but extrapolating from his 5k PB, he'd probably manage around 2:45 if he ran 26.2 miles without swimming 2.4 and cycling 112 beforehand.

Tim and I are still chatting as we reach the extensive halfway area; we both refuse the hot pasta on offer in favour of a banana and more salty purple squash, and keep going. The halfway point is always a rewarding moment in an endurance event: it means you can stop counting up and start counting down to the finish. So says Tim anyway, repeatedly, as we find we're still together as we jog towards the next aid station.

We don't ever decide to run the rest of the race together, we don't actually have that conversation, but over the course of the next few hours it becomes clear that we're in this together. I've never previously attempted to complete a race with someone else before, and never thought I'd want to. But I soon discover that it works remarkably well. As the distance begins to bite, you're not just inside your own head battling against those increasingly insistent negative thoughts. Instead, you're part of a team with the common goal of reaching the same (prodigiously distant) finish. Through aid station six (of nine), and I'm feeling fantastic as Tim nips into the bushes for a wee whilst I slow to a walk and phone my wife. She's busy with the kids but promises they'll all come to see me at the finish. Tim looks in all sorts of pain when he tries to get going again, like he's got cramp in both legs simultaneously, but somehow he pulls through.

I don't struggle until after mile 50. But when the hurt hits, it hits hard. In my stomach, in my thighs, calves, ankles and feet. Every footstep becomes an achievement. But crucially, having learned my lesson during the marathon stage of the Outlaw triathlon, I do remember to eat. However little I may feel like doing so, I force myself to pile in to everything on offer at the aid stations: sweets, granola bars, crisps, chocolate and squash, lovely squash. Today, I'm determined not to 'bonk'.

Bonking is what endurance athletes call running out of fuel. I bonked badly in Nottingham, quite apart from injuring my knee and calf. But not as dramatically as an Ironman triathlete called Chris Legh did, famously, in 1997. It was the World Championship in Hawaii and he was in fifth place just 50 yards from the finishing line. But suddenly he began staggering from side to side and try as he might, he simply couldn't stay upright. He collapsed by the side of Ali'i Drive, unable even to crawl the final few feet to the finish. He was carried away, and had DNF next to his name in the results list. Did not finish. I've resolved that won't happen to me.

So I eat, and eat. And eat. All day. And although my legs deteriorate badly in the final dozen miles or so, at least I still have some energy. By this time Tim seems to have got through the worst of his difficulties, so all I have to do is dig in and keep up. If I'd been on my own, I'd be tempted to walk a lot more than I do. But our agreement has always been to keep running, unless the gradient makes it counter-productive. At one point just after half way, we noticed we were barely gaining on another competitor who'd chosen to walk up a hill, but we were expending approximately double the energy by continuing to run. So when we see a steep enough slope, we walk. And we do find ourselves hoping, round every corner, for a sharp uphill. Because when you're running beyond 40 or 50 miles, slowing to a walk is like stepping into a warm bath of loveliness. All the pain instantly drains from your legs and stomach, and it feels like you're walking on air.

Starting to run again though, now that's tough. Again, if I'd been alone, with only the blisters, fatigue, soreness, spasms and doubt for company, I'd have probably taken a lot longer to summon up the willpower to get going again each time.

We pass a guy called Rich who's using this 62-mile race as his final training run for an upcoming 100-miler. That's the gold standard of ultra running it seems, 100 miles, and in some races those who complete the distance in less than 24 hours earn themselves a commemorative belt buckle. Tim and I decide that our current torments are more than enough to be going on with, and the 100-mile brigade can frankly keep their belt buckles.

Through the final aid station where they're offering the most delicious mini lemon tarts (yum, I'll definitely have another one of those, please), and back onto the Ridgeway where suddenly the finishing line becomes tangible. No more aid stations blocking the way, just seven more miles of stony path, then an ancient stone circle and the blessed relief of being able to stop running and stay stopped.

I'd never seriously doubted that I would get to the end, so the only real questions were how well would I finish? And how quickly? This second question pops up a lot, despite the fact I've been absolutely insisting (and still am) that a hilly ultra-marathon is categorically not about time. But because we're scheduled to finish a few minutes either side of the magical 12 hours, the barrier does seem to be occupying more and more conversation space the closer we get to the end. Tim has a support crew with him, in the shape of a pal he introduces to me as Big Foot (and who introduces himself to me as Marc). He's following our progress by charting the position of Tim's iPhone and driving to convenient points between aid stations to offer food, water and gels. I'll tell you something: we could all do with a pal like Big Foot/Marc.

Anyway, as we trot out of the final aid station, Marc's there too, warning that we're unlikely to break 12 hours at the current rate of progress.

Good, I think, *at least that's one less thing to worry about.*

Not good, says Tim, and speeds up.

So having spent 56 painful miles trying *not* to stress about time – indeed, having chosen a whole new type of running, having stepped up from road marathons to off-road ultras with the specific intention of *Not Stressing About Time* – I spend the entire final hour stressing about time. And love it.

For the entire final section we barely slow from the brisk pace Tim's setting and with two miles to go, we finally know we've cracked it. We're definitely going to finish inside 12 hours. I call for a final, ceremonial walk up a short, mild hill to celebrate and Tim agrees. I suspect he knows the real reason I'm asking is that I simply can't keep up without a quick rest. Then the dreadful sensation, for the final time, of starting to run again – and before long we've arrived at the ancient Avebury stone circle (which frankly we're both too tired to appreciate), around a field, and then a long straight path to the blessed finishing line.

I remember back to London Marathon a few months earlier, when people were encouraged to cross the line holding hands in honour of Dick Beardsley and Inge Simonsen, joint winners of the inaugural race in 1981. I suggest to Tim that we do the same. Running nine hours with the same person does tend to make you go a bit sentimental. And it was either that, or race.

We finish in 64th, which in a total field of over 2,000 feels great for a first effort. Then a hot dinner which never tasted so good. And in the car home, despite the vociferous protestations of wife and children, removing my shoes, which was definitely the best feeling of all. Because in my rush to get to the start, in my usual flurry of last-minute organisation, I'd made two extremely basic errors. First, it was only the night before when I realised the race was run east to west, away from London. I'd previously believed we were running towards the capital, and arranged to be picked up accordingly. Getting to Swindon was a much bigger logistical challenge for my family (as well as proving a much harder race for the runners, *into* a robust prevailing wind for fully 60 miles).

But the big mistake came as I rushed out of the front door early that morning. I forgot to bring my running shoes. Two pairs to choose from, but both the new trail running shoes and the lavishly cushioned road runners sat uselessly in the cupboard under the stairs as I stared out of the window of a bus on the M40 muttering furiously to myself. I was going to have to run in what I was wearing: a pair of tatty, long-ago retired trainers which were no longer even good enough to wear to the bottom of the garden. They were so old, the soles were coming loose, so battered they were about as cushioned as a pair of brogues, and so worn, they no longer felt like they ever might have fit. I get through a lot of trainers, and I'd only kept these because they were black, and look better than the usual light grey when worn under jeans.

The blisters began within the first mile of course, and grew steadily worse with every passing minute. After 11 and a half hours of off-road running in shoes almost as old as those ancient stones, my feet, once I'd managed to peel off my socks, looked like they'd been battered with a hammer. Still, totally deserved – what sort of fool forgets to bring running shoes to any race, let alone a first ultra? – and hopefully I've now learned my lesson.

Actually, make that *lessons*. The other one being – don't race a triathlon the day after your first ultra. Which is what I ended up doing on the Sunday in Derby, having promised Jenson Button I'd enter his excellent sprint tri, which raises money for Cancer Research UK. The swim was fine, really enjoyable in fact, and nice to be exercising at high intensity after a long day of slow jogging. The bike leg was also OK, if a little feeble. But the run wasn't half sore. In the middle of the previous night, I'd woken up starving and chosen to stay awake in bed knowing sleep was impossible without food, rather than suffer the pain of descending two flights of stairs to the kitchen on legs that were merrily seizing up.

And hours later, with my legs only getting worse, I found myself trying to sprint round a triathlon course. Great event, lovely atmosphere… terrible planning on my part.

Also in Derby, less than 24 hours after being absolutely convinced I would never take on anything longer than the Race to the Stones, and even as the post-race pain was at its peak, Tim and I began tentatively texting each other about that 100-mile belt buckle. I suddenly found myself determined to earn one. I mean 100 miles, it's the gold standard…

Speaking of which, the best analogy about ultra running arrived during that text exchange, courtesy of something Tim had just read on a forum.

'Ultra-marathons are like kids' parties. There's chocolate, cake, crisps, squash – and lots of silly running around.'

Scott Forbes

Winner of the Race to the Stones. A former professional triathlete, he's now a long-haul pilot for British Airways as well as a competitive athlete.

I remember being at prep school when I was about nine, being sent on punishment runs but actually loving it. This was when cross country was a punishment – and there was me enjoying it. I'd be sent on a run and I'd be thinking, 'This is great. I'm getting outside, I'm free', and I think the enjoyment side means you try a bit harder. I started competing when I was about 10, doing county stuff, and it just went on from there.

I got into triathlon when I was about 15, then went to Loughborough University, turned professional and spent about three or four years racing on the pro circuit trying to get into the 2000 Olympic Games at Sydney. Unfortunately, just before the Games I got injured and dropped out of the squad.

I needed a different direction, so went off and trained to be a pilot. Then when I was flying I didn't have enough time to do the three disciplines, so I focused on the cycling. I did quite well at that, winning national mountain bike titles and bits and pieces, but broke my neck in a bike accident and almost lost my life.

Too much metal work in my neck means I can't really cycle now, because if I have an accident then it's all over. So I've had to find a sport that would challenge me without being quite so dangerous and running was the obvious answer. I've always liked it, and I thought, 'Well, ultra-marathons seem to be the new mid-life crisis, so I'll give it a go'. And it turned out to be a good fit.

I'm loving it – loving the challenge, loving the diversity. No race is ever the same. If you do a 10k you start comparing yourself to your previous time and you're worrying about seconds and half seconds. There's no way you can compare an ultra-marathon with any course you've ever done before, or even the same course in a different year. Things are so different, so every time you compete, it's a new event, which is brilliant. You never get bored.

You go in with an intention of performing well but you have no idea how you're going to do until literally the last 10 minutes when you can really think to yourself, 'Right, this is how I've done', because anything could happen in these races. You can blow up half-way through, or get half an hour's lead before some guy comes through with five miles to go. It's so variable, you never know what's going to happen and I love that. You can't predict anything. You enter the race, take on the course, and you see how you feel at the end.

But being a pilot, and a new father, I find I have to be really quite ingenious to find time to train. For instance, I run every day, but I try and do it in the evenings, either on the treadmill or outside with a head torch. Sometimes I'll go out for lunch with my wife and afterwards she'll drop me 10 miles from home and I'll run back. Or if I'm getting my car serviced in town I'll drop it at the garage and I'll do a long run home then run back and pick it up later. I do a lot of my running when I'm abroad. I'll get changed at the airport, give my bags to another crew member to take on the bus and run to the hotel and meet them there. You work it into your life; you find out where you can fit training around what you would normally be doing. It's about being economical and clever.

When I won the Race for the Stones, I'd been getting time checks at the aid stations, and each time I got to a new checkpoint they'd say, 'You've got a 10-minute lead', and then, 'half-an-hour lead', and then with seven miles to go one lady told me, 'You've got an hour lead.' So I eased up a little and thought I wouldn't blow myself apart, I'd come in nice and easy. And as I was running down that final hill, coming off the ridge, turning right towards the farm, I looked over my shoulder and there was the second placed guy right on my heel, literally 50 yards behind me. And he was absolutely pacing it.

I thought 'Holy crap!' And just had to drop in my last two miles, down the hill to the farm, the loop round the stones, and then back up the way you'd come and into the finishing straight. I was doing six-and-a-half minute miles for those two miles. I had to really pull it out of the bag, so it actually turned into a sprint finish after nine hours. It was close, really close, and I loved that.

It was a great race, but I didn't know I had it won until I got onto that final straight towards the finishing arch. That was the only time in the entire race, the last 300 yards of a 62.2-mile race, that I could see him over my shoulder and thought, 'I've got enough of a lead to keep this.' For nine hours I hadn't seen anybody at all. I'd gone from the gun trying to blow everybody else apart. I'd known I was going quite well but then came the massive shock of seeing him tearing down the hill just behind me. Terrific race.

◉ The Beatles, *Run for Your Life*

'OUTLAW' iRONMAN TRiATHLON, MiLE 26

It's still surprisingly tough going, even though I can practically taste the finishing line. Actually, what I can practically taste is the posh burger I've promised myself as a reward. Big, rare and juicy in a fresh white bun with lots of ketchup and a nice cold lager. I've been contemplating this meal for months, have identified where in Nottingham I am going to get it, checked that they're open on a Sunday evening, and have even given up burgers for the past few months, just so it will taste better when I finally bite into it.

Then I see my children, Emily and Matthew, running towards me. Every time I've envisioned finishing over the past few hours, I was holding their hands as I crossed the line. They must have intuitively understood that for the final few yards I want them, no – more than that, I need them to be with me.

Because, you know, in a funny sort of way, this has been as much about Emily and Matthew as it has been about me.

Those long months of training, the thousands of lengths up and down the 20m pool in my local gym, the six-hour slogs on the bike to Box Hill through freezing wind and rain, the return home only to head straight back out for a run even though my legs felt like over-cooked spaghetti and my hands were too numb with cold to turn the key in the lock, let alone tie my laces – it was all building up to today, when I wanted to see if I could push myself to my very limits. And thanks to the somewhat shambolic way I've gone about race day – I've succeeded, at least, in that. Which is all that matters really. Not my finishing time; not what position I come. Just to push myself to my extreme, to be on the point of exhaustion, to know that all the pain goes away just by stopping, but then choosing not to stop, choosing to carry on.

Because the thing is, I felt I needed to do something like this to make the transition, in my own head, from boy to man. Even though I'm about to turn 40, until this day, until this moment, I've never felt like a proper grown-up. But I reckon it's about time to start. A boy can be a dad, but a man can be a father. So kids, this one's for you. And more than that, it's for your mum too. Caroline and I have been together since I *was* a boy (and she was a girl) but it's high time I grew up for her as well.

So as I approach the finish line, I know I'm changing. Ever so slightly, and probably nobody will be able to tell the difference – but to me, this is crucial.

I'd never swum in open water before today, never taken part in any swimming event come to that, never cycled with anyone else let alone as part of an organised race, and never, as a competitor, been anywhere near a triathlon.

So on some level, I knew that if I could get to the start line, and then at some stage during the day reach my physical limit and keep going, then I could also break down my mental barrier to turning 40. And it's worked.

Suddenly I don't much care if I'm not a young man anymore; in fact I prefer not to be, and I reckon I'm going to become a better husband and father, a better man, because of that.

As that thought takes shape, it's like I've downed a shot of strong contentment. Then, as always happens at the end of a race, even such a gruelling one, my legs get a second wind. Suddenly I feel like I can sprint to the finish. I try to do just that... and discover that I really can. I even have to slow down so the kids can keep up. This is what it's all about.

I really do love running. I think you've probably got that if you've read this far. It's the first thing I want to do if I have any time to myself – and the more the merrier. I also hope more and more people give running a go. The trend is definitely encouraging. The latest figures released by Sport England in 2015 show the number of people running at least once a week is up 63,000 to 2.1 million. The graphs for the rest of the UK are equally promising.

It's a far cry from the 1970s and '80s when I grew up and runners were viewed with mild pity. At primary school, I secretly used to enjoy the compulsory two-mile loop around the streets of suburban London during PE lessons. I would pretend not to. Everybody else was moaning on the way back to school, so I thought I'd better not admit that this running thing wasn't all that bad. Because back then, certainly at my school, saying you enjoyed running was equivalent nowadays to admitting a predilection for reading texts in Latin – a bit impressive, but a lot weird.

Then, by the time I got to secondary school all my energies were focused on avoiding sport and trying to be cool and rebel. What an idiot. I frequently wish I'd taken up running in my teens or at least in my twenties.

But perhaps it's for the best that I didn't. If I'd always run, I would doubtless have been less impressed by the simple power it has of transforming a life. I've watched with increasing pride as my two older kids have benefited from starting to run, reluctantly at first, but now gladly and willingly (or, in Emily's case, almost willingly). Their own stories come at the end of the final chapter, but I can honestly tell you it's one of the best things I've ever done for them. I look at their flushed faces at the end of our Saturday morning run, especially when they've done something cool like complete a first 10k or break the family parkrun record, and it makes me want to burst with pleasure. Neither of them is going to become a seriously good athlete, but that's totally not the point. They don't need to, or want to. They do need – and want – to be the best that *they* can be.

Same with me. Same with everyone. I'd never have been anything better than quite good. But since that first run ended embarrassingly with me wheezing against a lamppost a few hundred yards from my house, I simply became someone who fell in love with running, and stuck at it.

Running also enriches the lives of others around you. My kids are a case in point. So is my wife, who struggled for months for motivation to regain her fitness after the birth of our third child, but watched me and the kids go running together every week and thought, sod it, I want some of that. So she bought herself some new trainers and now looks fitter, leaner and even more gorgeous than she did in her twenties. There are also several people who work at Radio 2 who've been bitten by the running bug and look generally shinier and happier because of it. We've already heard from super-producer Graham.

I'm hoping that some of the UK's hardest to reach young people will be offered an introduction to this extraordinary sport as well. For several years now I've been an ambassador for a wonderful charity called SkillForce. They try to make a difference in the lives of young people most at risk of under-achievement or exclusion from school. Kids that for one reason or another look like they could be heading towards trouble. It's mostly ex-servicemen and women, who themselves can feel rudderless after leaving a career in the armed forces, who help these young people. I've seen them in action and they're inspirational.

Prince William is the royal patron and lends his name to the SkillForce award. He puts it like this. 'SkillForce does remarkable work with young people: the staff are predominantly ex-service men and women who use their extensive life experience and leadership skills to encourage pupils to stay engaged.'

Well, just recently I was having a coffee with the charity's chief executive Ben Slade and estimable director Liz Manning and we came up with the idea of the SkillForce Run in primary schools. Hopefully it will fast track some of that positivity around running into the people who need it most.

Every time it does that, it's a big win.

Ryan

I recently met Ryan whilst running over Hammersmith Bridge. He was coming the other way, round a buttress, and all of a sudden... crash! Skull onto skull, we were both knocked a little dizzy. We shot each other accusatory looks (his one to me was particularly menacing) but we seemed to realise simultaneously that this was nobody's fault. However, we did need a moment to recover, so as we sat overlooking the water on a convenient wooden bench built into the bridge, which I'd never noticed before, Ryan told me how he'd chanced upon running. It's a great tale, this. He agreed I could include it in the book as long as I didn't use his last name. Which, it occurs to me now, he never told me anyway.

I was in fights at school, lots of fights. Lots of other trouble. And then one day, just another fight, not even that bad, but this time they said, 'That's it, enough.' And chucked me out. Looking back, the way I was heading, I was maybe heading inside. I was angry all the time, looking for reasons to kick off and I didn't care about myself, or anything. Negative. Horrible. I live in the estate there and we've had problems with gangs. There was a stabbing a while back and at night you hear so much shouting.

Then my mate's uncle, he said I should try running with him. I didn't want to, it looked tough. It was tough, first time. I didn't have any proper gear so I just went in my normal clothes – my mate's uncle said that was fine. I'm glad I said yes. Couple of days later I went for a run by myself. Not long – just 10 minutes or something – but when I got back I realised I was pleased with myself, and maybe that was the first time, properly. It's like, when you've done something good, and feeling good not horrible, and after that you chase after the good feeling again. It made a big difference for me.

I'm running now three times a week. Four, maybe. One week I ran every day. And I'm much calmer, like my attitude has improved. It's like I respect myself, and if I feel respected then I'm OK. Also, it's shown me I can push myself and improve. Get faster and go further.

And now, I rarely ever even think about doing the same things that I was doing back then. It's like I'm running now, and I'm going the right way.

🔊 Queen, *Don't Stop Me Now*

'OUTLAW' iRONMAN TRiATHLON, FiNAL 385 YARDS

Past the marker showing 385 yards to go, and I think the kids are slightly regretting their decision to come onto the course and join me so early. I can see Matthew's mind working furiously as he tries to compute exactly how long a run he's let himself in for.

As both he and his sister Emily can tell, there's absolutely no way I'm letting go of their hands. I'm about to have my big cathartic moment, and I need them with me. In fact, I fully expected to be crying right now. I'm not a big crier generally, but over the past 12 hours, whenever I've thought about crossing the finishing line, whenever I envisioned what it would be like, I started welling up.

But now as it comes to it, with my beloved children alongside me, all I feel is deep contentment. This transcends happiness, transcends elation, transcends celebration. It literally does not get better than this. Except that it does. Because when it comes to it, the big cathartic moment I've been building up to simply isn't necessary.

We cross the line and I'm inspired to borrow the microphone from the tireless guy on the public address system. I find myself wanting to say a heartfelt thank you to the volunteers who've been magnificent all day: passing us water and gels, smiling, encouraging, applauding – all out of selfless altruism. I didn't plan to do it, and didn't really know what I was going to say when I grabbed the mic. But it's the perfect way to end an experience that's become too much about me. Thank you, everybody else. I couldn't have done it without you.

It's late afternoon in January and I'm running in Richmond Park with Holly the loony Labrador. She's carrying a stick the size of an average human leg and looking very pleased with herself for having found it. People who catch sight of her point and laugh, but she's oblivious to the mockery and laps up the attention. Her tail's wagging in windmills, and her nose is joyfully muddy from the recent exploration of a truly disgusting puddle. She's also just spent a happy half-hour running in and out of her favourite stream (it's where she found the stick). She's wet, she's muddy, she's out of breath, and she's struggling along with most of a tree in her mouth. Life, if you're Holly, simply does not get better than this.

As for me, I'm also covered in mud having tumbled over on a slippery slope. I've also just run through a huge, deep puddle and my left foot is both soaking and freezing. The icy cold has taken hold in my ears and fingers, and the biting wind is slicing straight through my supposedly windproof jacket. There's a low sun overhead temporarily blinding me, and I'm having to run faster than planned because I fear I may be late picking up my kids from school. Life, if you're me, simply doesn't get better than this.

As the poet Wendy Cope puts it (she's talking about an enormous orange, but it may as well have been running):

And that... made me so happy,
As ordinary things often do
Just lately...
This is peace and contentment. It's new.

All of which has got me thinking.

Here we have two mammals; both cold, wet and tired, but both as happy as happy can be. The canine has always enjoyed getting muddy and out of breath, but the human? Well, this feels like a revelation. Who could have guessed that a lazy, unfit smoker with a mild

Frazzles addiction could find such deep joy in such uncomfortable circumstances?

I'm not worried about the past, and I'm not fretting about the future. I'm simply in the moment. I am here, with this muddy dog, on this woody hillside, concentrating on where to place this next footstep among this unruly tangle of tree roots. The here and now. The journey not the destination. People spend lifetimes trying to achieve this state.

The thought occurs to me that I should commemorate this feeling because quite frankly, if I can find peace and serenity running in Richmond Park, anyone can. I'm sure that many of you reading this, those who really know how to run and who've been doing it all your lives, might despair at how much I still have to learn. You may be thinking *how dare he write a book about running?* And largely, I agree with you. I don't pretend to be an expert (though many of the people I've spoken to *are*) and I do of course know I'm not especially good at it. Having come to running relatively late, I've simply been struck by how brilliant it is. So I just wanted to celebrate that fact, and perhaps to inspire. That's why I asked 28 amazing people about their own routes into running. And if you haven't run in years, or indeed ever, do please just find some trainers and see where they take you.

Emily and Matthew

Emily had just turned 11 when she wrote this (every word of it). Matthew, who did the same, had just turned nine.

Emily

I never thought I could do sport. Once, on sports day, I cried because I thought I wasn't any good. I really REALLY didn't want to go for a run with my dad the first time, but he insisted. We tried to run alongside the river for one mile but I found it really hard to keep going without having a break for walking.

The next time I did manage the whole mile but I still found it tough. Actually, now I think about it, I really hated running when we started. Once, during a half term holiday, we went for a run and I almost cried again.

But after a while, we went to our first parkrun in Wimbledon Common. It's two muddy laps making up 5km and I thought the second one would never end. It was a fantastic moment when we did finish, me and my brother and our dad together, and for the first time I was proud of something sporty that I'd achieved. I could run 5km – epic!

Soon after that, I was surprised to be promoted to all the B teams at school, and then occasionally even to the A teams in netball and hockey. My sporting confidence grew and grew.

But then my younger brother beat my parkrun PB, and that was a big blow to my confidence. I sometimes dreaded going out running with my dad and Matthew on Saturday mornings. But then I realised that it doesn't matter who's quicker or who holds the family 5km record. I want to run fast and I want to do my best but I'm running my own race.

Running has helped in other ways too. I'm definitely more chilled out now. These days I can run a 10km race in less than an hour, and even though I don't always look forward to our weekend runs (sorry Daddy!), I do love the way it makes you feel afterwards. And I enjoy our celebratory croissants and doughnuts.

And there haven't been any more tears at sports day. In fact, during my final term at primary school, I won a medal in the long distance race!

Matthew

Like Emily, I found running hard to start with, but it taught me that if you work hard at something you can succeed.

At the beginning I only managed to get by because I knew I was struggling less than my sister. But then I realised I could actually do this, I'm quite fast and I can run a long way. I liked the way it made me feel afterwards. I like the way I try to overtake as many people as possible at the end of every race. We've done some great runs together, dad and me.

DON'T STOP ME NOW

Once we ran a 10k race together. It was really hilly and a bit tough, but I was the only kid running and I felt very proud at the finish.

As my dad told me after he finished an ultra-marathon, every run is a chance to learn little things about myself, and a chance to let myself shine.

Acknowledgements

A few kind folk to thank. First and foremost my wife Caroline. I mean I'm beyond grateful for everything anyway, but specifically for her help with this book during a holiday in France, for giving up almost every evening to read through the manuscript with me and suggest improvements. These 26.2 chapters would be a lot poorer if we'd stuck to our usual French regime and cracked open a bottle of rosé as soon as the kids were in bed. Thank you my darling, I really do appreciate it.

Thanks also to our three wonderful children, Emily, Matthew and Mary, who put up with an unusually distracted daddy as the deadlines loomed.

My heartfelt thanks to Chris Evans for a fantastic foreword and lots of encouragement. Chris was writing *Call the Midlife* at the same time as I was writing this, and there was nothing like finding out how few words I'd written by comparison to motivate me to get on with it.

Speaking of which, the help and support I received from the good people at Bloomsbury has been absolutely invaluable. Especially from Charlotte Croft, Sarah Connelly and Henry Lord. I knew nothing about the process of writing a book, so I truly appreciate all their advice and guidance along the way. It's been fun.

Also a massive thank you to all the people who gave up their time to be interviewed: experts, celebrities, successful sportsmen and women, and the bloke I bumped into (literally) on Hammersmith Bridge. There are 35 of you in total. So to the following people (in order of appearance) thank you, and I owe you a beer: Paula Radcliffe, Joss Naylor, Steve Cram, Mike Antoniades, Donovan Bailey, Paul Smith, Nicky Campbell, Angi Copson, Sally Gunnell, Noel Thatcher, Simon Kemp, Jenson Button, Jo Scott-Dalgleish, Chrissie Wellington, Andy Lane, Liz Yelling,

Martin Yelling, Nell McAndrew, Alistair Brownlee, Jonny Brownlee, Tom Williams, Helen Skelton-Myler, Rory Coleman, Claire Maxted, Allison Curbishley, Jo Pavey, Jennifer Bradley, Colin Jackson, Graham Albans, Richard Nerurkar, Greg Whyte, Scott Forbes, Ryan, Emily and Matthew.

And last of all, thank you to my two faithful running companions, Holly the Labrador (who never complains) and my injured left knee (which frequently complains but largely gets ignored). Both cover more daily miles than is probably good for them, I'm grateful that they stick with me.